Your Unlimited
Magnificent Memory

Your Unlimited Magnificent Memory

How to Improve Your Memory through Practical Creativity
- New, Fresh, Natural, Fun -

Robin J Constance

iUniverse, Inc.
New York Lincoln Shanghai

Your Unlimited Magnificent Memory
How to Improve Your Memory through Practical Creativity
- New, Fresh, Natural, Fun -

iUniverse books may be ordered through booksellers or by contacting:

iUniverse
2021 Pine Lake Road, Suite 100
Lincoln, NE 68512
www.iuniverse.com
1-800-Authors (1-800-288-4677)

ISBN-13: 978-0-595-33918-1 (pbk)
ISBN-13: 978-0-595-78708-1 (ebk)
ISBN-10: 0-595-33918-2 (pbk)
ISBN-10: 0-595-78708-8 (ebk)

Printed in the United States of America

My heartfelt thanks to:
Karen van der Merwe for
her page layout,
again and again;
Mark Wiggett for his apt and
fun-filled cartoons;
and
Thanks also to the professionals at iUniverse,
whose forbearance in the face of frightful fussiness
enables me to convey some thinking from my mind to many.

For a couple of years
—while I wrote most of this book—
we shared a life.
To Jill Bishop,
with love.

i have

magic memories

of two wonderful people

imaginatively called

Ma and Pa

thank you

yumm:

interj [ME *yummee,* fr. OF, fr. LL,

Gk *tummee,* modif. of Gk *tumm-,* *tummies,* lit. pleasant;

fr *tumescent*]; {child-talk alter. for *Hallelujah!*}—more at rhubarb,

alter. of *rha barbarum* lit., barbarian (15 C.)—originator befuddled:

a lovely warm feeling like Mum and peanut butter.

Yumm:

Your Unlimited, Magnificent Memory.

Every one of us is made up of two parts: our material body and our 'immaterial' mind; the one an indivisible aspect of the other. Of itself your mind has no physical strength whatsoever, yet it is an awesome demonstration of greatness, of power and purpose. A manifestation of EnergyWorld; your mind enables you to look backwards to your past, relate this to your present and significantly determine your future.

Each on a matter of the mind, *Your Unlimited, Magnificent Memory* is the first book in a series of three. Between them, the three books span the sequence of every life: what was, what is and what will be.

The second is *Universal, Mighty Mind*. This book explores the greatest force in your creation…your very own arrangement of cosmic energies: your mind. The message of *Umm* is simple: you *should* have it all otherwise a thrifty Universe would not have given you all the gear. Just as the Sun has all it needs to shine; you can have it all because the equipment necessary is already an integral part of you: a mind to be, a body to do and a natural desire to have. If you want intensely and do persistently, a whole new life of singular happiness shall be yours; Not can be; shall be. This is a cosmic guarantee, underwritten by your universal, mighty mind and assured by your being in the immediate present.

So U Magnify, Maestro—the third in the trilogy—focuses on your mind's most powerful attribute: your creative imagination. Your inborn ability to bring about in advance enables you to be infinitely more than just the *sum* of your parts. This book shows you how to be at one with yourself by discovering what is most important to you—figuring out what you're really about—and getting on with the business of being it. Living as 'the-true-you' is the wellspring of your enduring joy; there can be no other origin. For the time of your life, *Summ* will help you design your own genuinely glee-filled future.

Your Unlimited, Magnificent Memory—the first in the trilogy—hones in on your mind's most important attribute; the one on which all your living depends: your capacity to recall. This book shows you how to bring any information (including names and numbers) back to tongue-tip instantly and effortlessly…to remember beyond your wildest imaginings, to recapture your past.

But *Yumm* is more than a how-to for recollecting. It is designed to make you more conscious of mind and memory and to help you take more active control of your thought processes. Conscious memory is not an island unto itself. It is an integral, vital aspect of mind. To develop memory is to enlarge and expand the whole mind. *Your Unlimited, Magnificent Memory* is inspiring, liberating, expansive…

Umm thrives in today, *Summ* envisages a shining tomorrow. And yesterday?…

Welcome to your panoply of memories.

Welcome to *Yumm.*

Contents

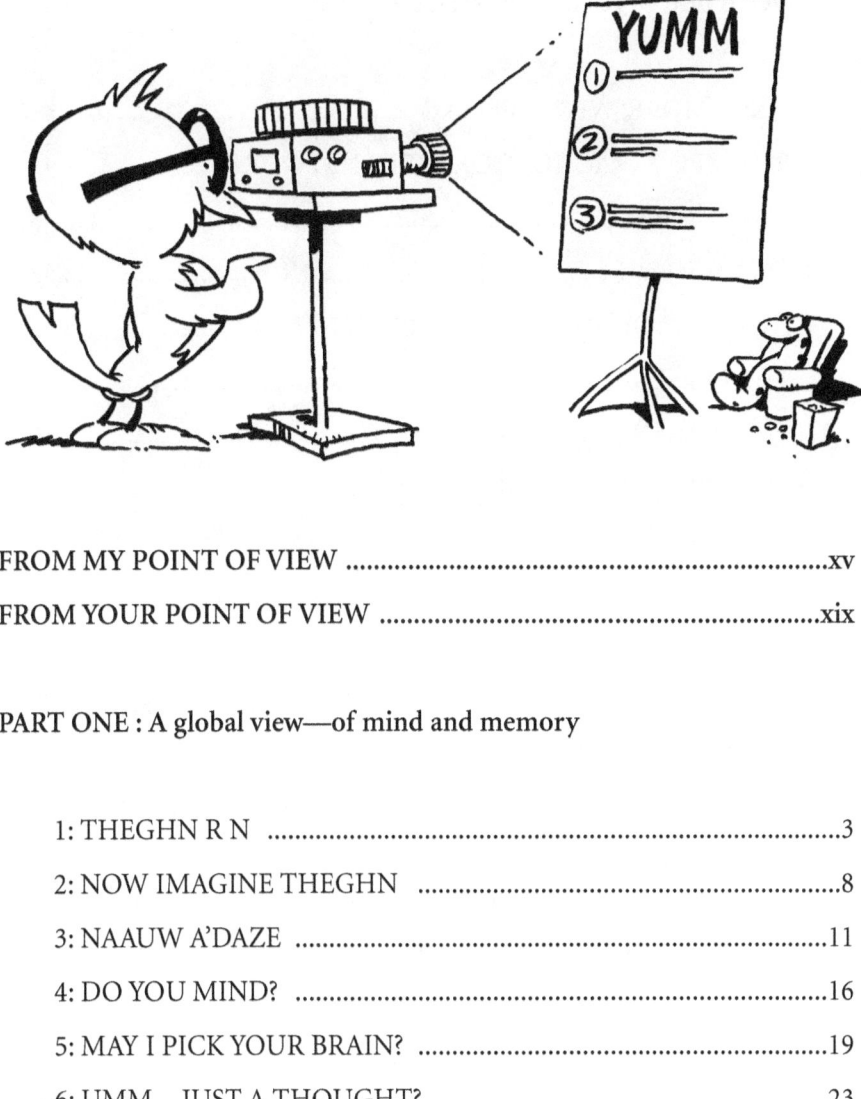

PART TWO: A bird's-eye view: the six GUTs of memory

PART THREE: A worm's-eye view: specific tools and techniques

FROM MY POINT OF VIEW

Dear Reader,

Life is about people, and taking care of change. We are human beings. The vibrant essence of "being" is mind, and the warm, throbbing heart of mind is memory. Whoever you are, at whatever age or stage, your unlimited magnificent memory is the bedrock on which you rely. We all have an unlimited capacity to bring information back to tongue-tip instantly and effortlessly. With *Your Unlimited, Magnificent Memory* (*Yumm*) you can learn to remember beyond your wildest imaginings.

These days we demand more of life than mere survival. We need to be happy and fulfilled. This means that we all have to learn, grow, and develop—and this process is ongoing, for life. With *Your Unlimited, Magnificent Memory* you will grow as a person and develop as an individual. This is why I have written *Yumm*—in order to carry you to the farthest reaches of self-confident enjoyment and energetic well-being. The journey will be magnificent. You will thrive.

We are all able to learn a physical skill, such as driving a car, cooking, or playing golf, and we are also adept at developing that talent. Can we develop a mental gift? Of course we can. We have a natural capacity to live more proficiently, on both the physical and the mental levels. All accomplishments start in mind, anyway. A muscle cannot move itself. The body needs instruction, and that comes from *mind*: the wellspring of all that we are.

It is ironic that those people who want to improve their memory are often the ones who say, "Nothing can help me." If they hold that belief, they are right: Nothing can or will help them, because they will not allow anything to. They are truly prophetic in that they predict failure—they expect it. So they do fail, "successfully," every time!

How did I become interested in the process of remembering? Soon after I turned forty, I chose to have a complete career change. I needed to educate myself further and acquire new skills. I did courses in real estate, sales techniques, and financial management. Time passed, but I did not feel either sharp or confident. I needed to know why, so I continued to dig deeper by asking questions, questions, and yet more questions. Even the most basic queries led me inevitably back to memory. This vast treasure-store of information, which should be freely retrievable, is our indispensable source of reference—our database.

I do not think of myself as an expert. Though I have been around for more than fifty years, I'm still just an inquisitive kid at heart. I don't have any "acceptable" tertiary qualifications or "appropriate" formal training. My bachelor's degree is a legal one from an obscure, but superb, little university near Africa's foot. So if you want a dull tome, a scientific paper, or loads of psychobabble, you're looking in the wrong place. In this book there is no jargon or technotalk; I don't know any. But this lack of the so-called "right" credentials cuts two ways. It also means that I have no bias or prejudice, no inclination to prove this or confirm that. I have explored memory with an open and receptive mind. I have been free to be me.

In fairness, I have enjoyed much acclaim as a memory trainer to everyday people, teams, and leaders, including some of the most senior members of ex-President Nelson Mandela's cabinet while he was still in office. Further, these private coaching sessions, as well as more public seminars, formed the foundation for my ever-popular talks and sellout programs on Possibility Thinking and Life Success, both in Southern Africa and Britain.

Yumm is designed to be a useful working tool—your own personal seminar, a guide for learning about and using your memory effectively. Very little of the material is original. Over the last few years I have scoured the popular literature in the libraries and bookshops, and browsed fold-up tables groaning under the weight of old, discarded books at pavement sales and morning markets. I have ferreted out books from dusty old antiquarian stores, mooched through garages, and rummaged through attics and basements. I have watched others, and using that uniquely human attribute of self-consciousness, I have watched myself. This *little red book* is a distillate of the most practical and useful ideas and techniques.

Heightened consciousness occurs when one lives more deliberately and with greater appreciation, because each life should be a voyage of self-discovery, of learning more about oneself. *Yumm* will compel you to be more conscious. Not only will you observe more, but all your senses will become more acute. You will make more sense of the world, literally. You'll become more sensitive and more alert. You will learn to focus on one thing at a time, without distraction. Put another way, you will gain more control of your thoughts. Thinking is the highest sphere of mind, and mind is the essence of all that we are.

We all learn to function effectively by experiencing success. As you develop your inborn capacity to bring information back to mind, you will expect to remember whatever you choose. You will learn to trust your memory and believe in its staggering power. Your own improved ability to recall will serve as your inspiration. This cycle of positive expectation will feed on itself. An unshakeable confidence will gradually permeate your entire being.

If you are willing to try new things, see with fresh eyes, look at old skills differently, and consider things from another angle, then pride in your own accomplishments will enfold you, irresistibly carrying you farther and higher. Increasingly you will enjoy your ever-improving memory. With some new habits of thought, you will be a bigger person. Living will become a fuller and more worthwhile adventure as you expand your mind and enrich your life.

Yumm is a most powerful tool. As soon as you understand the methods and systems, use them. You will remember more, starting immediately. That is a cosmic guarantee, underwritten by your very own universal, mighty mind.

Have fun!

Robin Constance

P.S. There are surprisingly few books on memory out there in the marketplace. This is doubly astonishing because memory is such a vitally important aspect of each and every one of us, and it is of such universal interest.

Yumm is different from the usual memory book. In addition to being a "why" and "how-to" book, it is also designed to be its own practical work manual. As a result—early on and then continuously throughout its pages—you will bump into some strange presentations: GUTs, B4s, *ruts,* and other ongoing oddities! This is because I am actually using the tools and techniques that I recommend. As you move through the text, you will be able to judge for yourself the effectiveness of many of the methods and to get instant feedback on what works for you. The various tools and techniques are summed up in the second-to-last chapter (28): "And these are the tools the *Wise Ones* use".

FROM YOUR POINT OF VIEW

Yumm is divided into three sections:

Part One is a global view to develop your consciousness of the concepts of mind and memory; it is the big human picture from a distant, detached perspective. I also want you to focus your thinking on the notion of your own unlimited, magnificent memory, probably for the first time in your life.

As I became interested in the process of remembering, I wanted more than memory aids and effective techniques. I needed to know more about memory in its widest sense. I felt compelled to think more about my ultimate question: What has enabled you and me to stand at the pinnacle of known intelligent life? This raised many, many new questions: What is the relationship between brain and mind? Indeed, what is mind? Why is mind the fundamental essence of all that we are? How are mind and memory interlinked? What is memory? Why is our ability to recall so vital to our very functioning? How do we deliberately retrieve information? Why is memory our most important faculty?

In this first section, my intention is to create and develop your consciousness. First, so you become conscious of the universal, mighty realm that is your mind. Second, so you think about and reflect on your unlimited, magnificent memory.

Part Two is a bird's-eye view about understanding the principles behind the process of effective remembering.

Recollecting is an internal and invisible process, based on six principles that I call the Great Universal Truths the GUTs of memory. These GUTs are valid for all, forever. They are a timeless certainty. These great universal truths are reliable; they are fixed, unchangeable, and fundamental. We can depend on them. To learn and apply these simple verities is fun and effective. They are easy to grasp, and the results are practically instantaneous. If you truly know the why and the what, you will persist with the how.

Part Three is a worm's-eye view—the how—that provides specific tools and techniques for improving day-to-day remembering.

The *Sound System* will help you remember numbers. First devised some 350 years ago, this system has been repeatedly improved. Nevertheless, I have introduced a number of refinements that include expanding the basic unit of memory from two to four digits. This is a quantum leap forward. The Sound System has another huge advantage: It is an ideal structure for developing your natural ability to think innovatively, because your creative imagination is your most powerful faculty.

Because this method is both sophisticated and versatile, it takes some effort to master. In chapter 19, I explain the rewards to be had from the Sound System. I cover the System itself in chapters 20, 21, and 22, but if they look too daunting, skip them. You can always come back to them at a later stage when you are more comfortable with the rest of the material.

In this section, there are also chapters on recognizing faces and remembering names, the causes of and cures for absentmindedness, and my thoughts on memory and advancing years.

A summary of general methods and techniques that are indispensable to effective remembering wraps up Part Three.

PART ONE

A GLOBAL VIEW— OF MIND AND MEMORY

1

Theghn R N

Let's call him Theghn. The "gh" is silent, as in *thought*. So his name is pronounced *Then*, and he's a contented fella.

As usual, he'd awakened just before sunrise. For the last few cycles of day and night (what we would know roughly as months), he would have curled up tighter, trying to keep some warmth against the freezing dark air. But now the season was well into a time of rebirth. When the sun was at the base of the valley, still low above the horizon, he stretched and rose. On his way out of the sleeping area, Theghn scraped the congealed remains of the previous evening's meal into his mouth and walked on. Then he paused, belched, and clambered on up the hill, where an enormous rock jutted out from the cliff face.

With the assurance of deep familiarity, Theghn walked to the tip of the dark-brown boulder and sat down. He saw his companion, Ago, moving around in the living area below. They had stayed together for a long time. She had produced many children, a few of whom were still alive, fit, and strong.

Theghn was well-satisfied with his lot as he regarded the view from his vantage point. Very little existed for him, apart from the valley and a small part of the plains beyond that he knew. He and all his clan had been born there. So had their fathers, and their fathers before them. They all felt secure in this tiny area. It was safe and predictable. After all, existence was survival in the longer term, so reproduction was the ultimate aim of existence. And so he continued just to sit.

From the perspective of today, with our love for abbreviations, we might well have dubbed our hero "Theghn R N." But the R N would not have stood for Registered Nurse or Royal Navy. Theghn, Ago, and their clan lived long before such sophisticated titles existed. This scene took place 30,000 years ago, and R N stands for "Reflective Neanderthal."

Dim impressions of a recent event were drifting through Theghn's head...

A few sunrises before, an enormous boar had been spotted in the valley. The presence of so large a pig was most unusual, and such an opportunity could not be lost. The succulent meat would be a rare and tender treat. Just as important, killing so challenging a quarry would revitalize the cooperative energies of the tribe and strengthen bonds of kinship and community.

The day before the hunt, a coffin-shaped pit had been dug, the depth of a man standing, along each of the three main paths that ran down the valley. At the bottom of each hole, six strong, sharpened poles had been driven point-up into the ground. A light skeleton of trimmed branches had been placed carefully over the open mouth of the cavity and spread with sand, gravel, and brush to hide the brutal stakes.

On the morning of the hunt itself, the women and children had made their way a short distance up the valley along a cliff path. Then they had spread themselves abreast across the width of the valley. The able-bodied men had hidden themselves around the concealed pits. The thick, tangled undergrowth had made it difficult to position themselves precisely, but this natural obstruction would force the enormous boar, with his huge tusks, to travel along one of the three paths that led down the valley. Once away from these tracks and into the open plains, the boar would have been safe.

For the three waiting groups of men, the tension levels had risen. Nothing had happened for over an hour. The great rock jutting from the cliff face cast its long shadow, and when this shade reached a prearranged spot, one of the women began screeching. This was the signal for which they had all been waiting. The rest of the women and all the children began shouting and screaming as they tried to drive the beast down the valley. The dignified harmony of the area had been reduced to loud confusion.

Over many years of survival the huge hog had acquired both bulk and strength. He had also learned a formidable cunning. To escape the confining undergrowth, the pig at first veered onto one of the main paths and charged down toward safety beyond the valley. Then he must have sensed the presence of the hunters, for he did not continue to dash headlong down the track toward the gruesome fate prepared for him. Instead, he climbed up the side of the valley by way of a shallow gully, reached thinner vegetation at the base of the cliff wall, and raced along toward the plains. But his escape was blocked by a ridge that descended from the base of the towering cliff clear down to the path.

So the boar suddenly appeared out of the densest forest above his would-be slayers—the party led by Theghn. This was a commanding position for the beast; his left flank was fully protected by the rocky spine. He also enjoyed two other tactical advantages: the high ground and total surprise.

Theghn's hunting group was thrown into instant disarray. Their prey was upon them—vicious, maddened, and lethal. Despite the pit with its grisly spikes; their needle-sharp, stone-tipped spears; their muscle and their numbers, the men suffered terribly. The group could not act flexibly or efficiently, for the men were not capable of thinking as part of a team. Further, both their memory and their imagination were severely limited. In another way, too, the hunting party was desperately ill-equipped to face the deadly force confronting it. Theghn and his men could not talk to each other.

A mere 30,000 years ago, an eye-blink in the evolution of our species, language had not been invented.

When did this new type of creature called *Homo sapiens* emerge? At what stage did Thinking Man arrive? He is, after all, the predecessor of you and me. The answer depends largely on how we define *human*. What is the key? Is walking upright on two hind legs the clincher? Is it brain size? Tool-making abilities?

Conventionally, our direct ancestors are considered to be the ones who had the mental capacity to make and use tools systematically. A tool is merely something we employ to make life easier and better, preferably both. Our first tools were simple points and crude edges made by hitting stones together. They probably saw the light of day for the first time some two to four million years ago.

It was the success of these early tools, elementary and crude as they were, that accelerated the whole trend of human development. They led to the complex societies and diverse civilizations of today. To say that humans invented tools is, at best, a half-truth. It would be more accurate to say that tools invented humans. Each new invention, each refinement to an existing device, expanded the human brain. So better gadgets led, slowly but surely, to better brains, which in turn spawned better tools. And so evolution—the process of gradual growth and development into more and more complex living things—stumbled ponderously forward.

Consider Theghn's behavior when we met him that balmy spring morning. His inner, mental life—in contrast to his inner, physical workings—was based purely on sensation, a sort of hazy, foggy "feeling-feeling." Without language he was not able to think—to string ideas together in a deliberate flow for a purpose. So his memory—being able to recall past feelings, thoughts, and knowledge—would have been blurred, woolly, and rough. And his imagination—the ability to picture more than what was actually happening to him—would have been very limited, ill-defined, vague, and misty.

Neither Theghn nor any of his clan would have been able to consider hunger or to ponder pain, to judge the hardness of a rock, to contemplate the softness of a breast, to reflect on the nature of calmness, to mull over the feeling of serenity, to imagine wellness or well-being, or to visualize health. He would have been a body primarily controlled by a physical thing: his brain. More advanced than any other species on this planet, our ancestor Theghn was still light years away, mentally, from you and me.

Over generations, the fuzzy "feeling-feelings" of Theghn grew into language. First, everyday things became recognizable through specific sounds. This was the origin of a system for communicating with others, based on sounds combined into words. Then ideas were given the same treatment. They acquired *sound tags,* verbal labels that were in turn, arranged in sequence. Coherent thought was arriving, for thinking is about purposeful mental structuring. Within a deliberate and considered framework, we learned to exchange thoughts effectively. All this progress was both a cause and an effect of language.

Language makes you and me human; it gives us the handles with which we grasp our world. Through language, we can exchange information with other people. This code, language, uses a store of words—our vocabulary—that encapsulate meaning. But language is more than just a collection of meaningful words lumped together. There is another equally vital aspect: grammar. We learn to use words in a particular order. The training we undergo to grasp this system requires organization. With language, communication is no longer just a limited series of hoots and howls, or grunts, groans, and gestures.

Two interdependent faculties separate us from all other life: our ability to *think,* and our ability to *communicate* what we are thinking. Language and thought, thought and language stand massive in the story of humankind, in our story.

Along with language and thought, method and system were essential for the evolution of our unlimited, mighty mind. With mind came the genesis of modern man.

And the warm, pulsating heart of mind is memory.

2

Now Imagine Theghn

Right now I need your attention. I would like you to do something truly stupendous. Stupendous? Yes, something wonderful, astounding, huge.

Just focus your attention for a couple of seconds on *stupendous*. Not only is it a long word, but it is also gargantuan, colossal, massive, and titanic in its meaning. This is dramatic stuff. I am going to ask you to do something—something that separates you from every other living thing on this planet, apart from your fellow humans, of course.

And it is something that you do countless times every day! Yet you have probably never given it so much as a passing thought. This time you are going to do it deliberately. You will be conscious of your mental processes, of your thinking…

Lose yourself for a few moments in that last berserk, panic-filled fiasco with Theghn, his men, and the maddened boar. Create in your mind the screams of pain, the fiendish confusion as tusks and spears ripped flesh in that terrifying melee of spattering body fluids. Feel the fear; smell the blood; hear the grunts and the sound of tearing tissue.

Suddenly you are lying on your back, pinned to the ground by the enraged pig. His maniacal eyes stare directly into yours. He wants death—your death. Uncaring, unthinking, desperate, you sink your teeth into his mucus-filled nostril. You have the nose of a raging wild pig in your mouth. Taste it. Feel the pressure as it tries to rip free. Your jaw stays locked to the frenzied muzzle as it thrashes back and forth, whipping you this way and that. Hear his demented screeches in your ear. Sense your revulsion.

Let go.

The boar pulls away but continues to glare with crazed menace into your terrified eyes. A few drops of frothy blood from his soft, torn snout drip onto your upper lip. Experience your disgust. You are overwhelmed by his foul, steaming breath. Pause and imagine that vile stench as the rest of your body thrashes violently in the dust and mayhem of that little forest clearing.

Go on, dear reader, there is good reason. Just do it—swim freely, totally immersed, in the morbid depths of those few ghastly moments…

You have been fully involved in a life-and-death battle. As you lay on the ground, fighting for your life, your whole being was centered on two faces: yours and the boar's. Every cell in your whole body, each iota of intelligence that animates your entire being, was confined to that tiny corner of reality. Life itself was reduced to two faces: the hog's and yours. For all practical purposes, nothing else existed. Your perspective of the incident was very restricted. Your universe was as limited as that of a caterpillar. You had a worm's-eye view of what happened.

Now stay with that event, but stop being personally involved. Pretend that you were a small bird, a robin perhaps, sitting high in a nearby tree and watching this violent scene. As a disinterested observer, you were able to see the drama unfold. From the behavior of the pig, the nature of the terrain, and the actions of the hunting party, you were able to deduce that an awesome battle would take place. You could understand and appreciate the wily tactics of the boar. You were able to predict the fierce fury and the carnage that ensued. Your safe and secure perch was an ideal spot to observe what was happening. From your detached perspective, you could have seen the big picture. You had a bird's-eye view of the whole affair.

And so you had three choices: You could get involved at a fundamental level (a worm's-eye view), or you could be detached and get an overall impression (a bird's-eye view), or you could ponder the whole event in the context of Theghn and the tribe, their entire world (a global view—a very broad perspective).

Actually, there was a fourth choice: Avoid the whole thing by simply flying away (no view at all).

So what stupendous feat have you just performed? You have just been on a limitless flight of pure creative imagination—the ability to experience beyond what is actually happening to you. Imagination is based on conscious memory—stored information that you can recall at will. Feeling and thinking enabled you to use both your imagination and your memory.

Man's most *important* attribute is
memory.
Man's most *powerful* attribute is
imagination.
The *force* that *fuses* these two is
thinking and feeling.
These are the three main pillars of *mind*,
and mind is the sum and substance of you and me.

3

Naauw A'Daze

Let's come forward 30,000 years, and meet Naauw A'Daze. Her first name is pronounced *Now*. She is Modern Man: perceptive, sensitive, and aware.

She decides to clamber to the tip of the dark-brown boulder, the same one that Theghn sat on so long ago. With a caution born of deep-seated fear of the unknown, she picks her way slowly along the unfamiliar surface. Halfway, she stops altogether. Hesitantly she lowers herself to sit astride the rock, her legs swinging on either side. Naauw is unsure of how to go on, but she is determined and organized in her thinking. With her hands open and palms facing down, wrists touching and fingers extended, she inches forward until she reaches the end of the rock.

Looking straight down past her hands, she sees the sides of the valley fall steeply away to the river far below. She feels as if she is supported in space. Naauw had issued herself a challenge (to sit at the tip of the great boulder) and set herself an objective (to gain the most breathtaking view possible). The thrill of the double achievement banishes the negative and pervasive tension of seconds ago. Her mood changes instantly. Naauw is elated by her two small victories. Once again, she has shown the power of her belief: *If it's to be, it is up to me.*

The gentle orange on the horizon is fast giving way to a bright, clear blue over-head, lit by the serene and powerful yellow of the sun's brilliance. The valley itself is a tapestry of various greens that make up the fertile forest, ringed by stark, harsh cliffs. In the riot of organized color, she can feel the excitement as life everywhere greets the new day. She watches brightly colored birds flitting frenetically on their self-important missions. Naauw sees enormous, vulture-like creatures on their early-morning warm-up flights, soaring high above the valley floor. She glimpses the white-tipped flicker of an alert antelope's ear as it trips noiselessly through the undergrowth beneath her. And so she continues just to sit, and daydream.

Naauw feels at peace with herself and her life. This part of the world is completely new to her, but she welcomes the newness. To her this scene is stunningly beautiful. Her mood is happy and relaxed, confident and serene. Her thoughts drift easily, flowing from one idea to another. If she stopped to analyze her dreaming, she would realize that no idea or thought can exist alone. Each must always be linked or associated via memory with another bit of knowledge. For no apparent reason, the flicker of the antelope's ear leads her to thoughts of her ancestors: "Who were they? Where had they lived? What happened to them? How had they hunted these graceful animals?"

Memory and imagination allow Naauw to create, without effort, a clear mental impression of an imagined hunt. She can actually experience a fabrication of her mind. Naauw sees a vivid montage. There is the sound of stone thudding and jarring on bone, the sensation of a tusk ripping flesh. She hears yells, shouts, and screams; tastes splattered blood; smells sweat; senses disarray and triumph; and feels the joy of victory and the quiet of despair. The whole ghastly scene becomes real. In her mind, she has created something alive. This is stupendous! Naauw shivers.

But the setting is too tranquil for her to dwell on violent thoughts of hunting. Her thoughts drift on. Would her forebears, those many years ago, have been able to appreciate the dignified majesty of the world around them? The easy harmony of her mood leads her to study the enchanting tranquility of her surroundings.

She is a gifted painter, so her senses are attuned to the delicate tones of green. She notices much, much more than another person would. Her powers of observation are sharp, and her mind is piercing, subtle, and keen. Through a developed combination of eyes and mind, she perceives the scene around her with extraordinary vividness. Naauw lives at a higher level of consciousness and sensitivity, so she experiences more than most people. She participates more actively and fully in the vast and wonderful process of living.

After a while Naauw's musing is interrupted by the sight of her husband, Yest, moving around on the grass below. She wonders about his family—his sister Marie and his brother who died in the war. That was an amazing man, much loved and respected by all. "What was his name?" It doesn't come to mind. There is no mental picture, no image, no recall—nothing. A minute trace of irritation enters Naauw's otherwise pleasant thoughts.

"What was his name?" A blank and definite displeasure. She puts the question to herself again and frowns. Her brow furrows as she tries to will the answer from an uncooperative memory. "I know you're there," she says to herself. "I know your name almost as well as my own. Come on out!"

She tries to coax the information to the surface, but to no avail. That trifling fact simply eludes her, and the harder she tries, the more it seems to slip away. Anxiety and tension are the enemies of remembering. Forgetting thrives in a state of tension and anxiety.

At first she feels acute annoyance, and then she reacts typically: "Bloody memory, it always lets me down. I'm only human and a typical woman—can't remember a thing. And the older I get, the worse it gets!"

Seconds before, her thoughts and her mood had been confident and relaxed. But now cracks are appearing in her contentment. Despite the wealth and complexity of the information she has brought to tongue-tip instantly and effortlessly, Naauw is irked by this tiny piece of missing material. Instead of enjoying the staggering gifts that her memory has freely given her, she is frustrated because she cannot find the equivalent of a single drop in a vast ocean. Her sense of perspective is completely lost.

Such anger might seem unusual in one so competent. Sadly, a response like this is all too common.

Naauw is very conscious of activity at the physical level, but somehow she takes the most basic mental skills for granted. This is not deliberate; she is just not conscious of her ability to remember. She simply doesn't think about it. The only time she might be conscious of her memory, for a few fleeting seconds, is in a situation like the one she is in at present.

Sometimes she goes to the other extreme. Instead of berating her memory for letting her down every time, she'll brag about its uselessness. She'll say, "My memory is a disaster area. Bad, and getting worse. A nemesis on the premises. An accident waiting to happen. First signs of Alzheimer's. Early senility. In one ear and out the other. The thing I use to forget with. Can never remember a thing, you know. Memory? What's that?"

What we say to ourselves can be an awesome force, especially if we accept our words as true, because mere mental meanderings have crystallized into beliefs.

All too often, we assume that such firm convictions, such beliefs, will be true in the future. By then they have become expectations, and expectations are an almighty power. In fact, our lives in general are a self-fulfilling prophecy—the realization of our beliefs, or more specifically, our expectations.

Let me repeat: We invented words to express our thinking. What we say is usually what we believe, and what we believe is what we'll probably get.

We all need the love and loyalty of our families, the closest and most intimate support group that we have. Imagine how you would feel if your loved ones consistently and persistently talked about you and treated you as irresponsible, unworthy, inept, and incompetent—a sad joke.

Until now, how have you talked about (either to yourself or others) and treated your very own memory? Did you

<u>B</u>lame?	"It's all *your* fault. *You* failed me, again."
<u>B</u>elittle?	"What can you *expect* from something so *untrustworthy*?"
<u>B</u>erate?	"Can't it *ever* do *anything* right?"
<u>B</u>rag?	"Here comes good ol' scatterbrain. Reliable as ever!'"

Those are the four deadly sins of memory: **the four Bees—the 4Bs**—as they were **B4—be-fore**—before you started out on *Your Unlimited, Magnificent Memory*. They are now **the four not-to-bees**—no blaming, no belittling, no berating, and no sardonic bragging.

At this stage, dear reader, so as not to offend me, you might want to ask gently: "Robin, isn't this **B4** thing a little, sort of, well, you know…er, childish? A bit corny?"

"Yee-yupp, sure is," I would agree readily, and then I would immediately pose another question:

"But has it got the idea of honoring your memory to stick in your mind?"

"Uh huh…I guess so. I won't forget it," you would hopefully reply.

"So has it made my point memorable?"

"I guess so."

That's my sole intention.

The fundamental feature that separates you and me from cauliflowers and roses, rocks and rock pigeons, is mental. We call this formless, invisible, dimensionless realm "mind." Your memory is a crucial member of your mental household. Your ability to remember is, as you will recall, the most *important* aspect of your mind. Revere your memory.

From now on,
henceforth and forevermore,
you will give your memory
ongoing **respect, trust,** and **encouragement.**
You will **support** your memory with **love**
by design
on purpose
consciously
deliberately
with intention
in cold blood
for life.

So it is written, so shall it be done.

(If this is the only wise counsel you get from *Yumm,* this book will have paid for itself many, many times over.)

4

Do You Mind?

Being human, Naauw belongs to the most successful animal species that has ever lived. This means that you, too, are a celebration of that unique success story. Building your life to the point where you are now has taken immense brain power. And you are unstoppable. No sooner do you encounter a new problem than you set about solving it. In so doing, you drive yourself relentlessly to a higher level of achievement. You are an unequalled celebration of mind.

Your ancestor, Hunter Theghn, survived on a diet of fruit and roots. Physically, you have hardly evolved at all since those days. Despite your car and your computer, your tools and all your technology, your body remains much the same as those of Theghn and Ago. Thirty thousand years have not made much difference, at least not on the outside.

Don't be fooled by Theghn's simple behavior. His brain was staggeringly complex. By challenging the boar, he and his men stuck their necks out, and a couple of heads were chopped off. However, Theghn was a leader and always striving to improve. His brain constantly clawed and grasped to get beyond the actions needed for bleak survival. The insatiable curiosity, fierce intelligence, and innate enthusiasm of his brain groped ever onward, ever upward. The next major breakthrough of Theghn's species was the birth of thinking, and so his descendants developed language.

Gradually, as knowledge and experience grew, the day-to-day problems of merely staying alive became fewer and fewer. At some stage, our ancestors thrust themselves through the survival barrier and into a new way of life, where they had extra time and energy to create a freer, less hostile environment. We became the only creatures able to overcome, to alter, to manipulate, and to dominate the world around us. We alone can live actively by choice, not just passively by chance. Only Man can proactively and deliberately choose to thrive.

We exploit and expand every nook and cranny of our brain's capabilities. Theghn's narrow little hunting ground became Yest's huge sporting arenas and stadiums. The simple, shallow pit in which Ago was buried led to the Great Pyramids of Giza and that dazzling marble mausoleum outside Agra, the Taj Mahal. The crude cave home of the clan was the forerunner of our office towers, the Manhattan and Hong Kong skylines, and other building triumphs—St. Peter's Basilica in Rome, the Forbidden City in Beijing, the Kremlin in Moscow. The deeper yearnings of Theghn evolved into the literature and theatre, music and painting, and wit and humor of Naauw. The civilizations and cultures of our species evolved from crude beginnings.

The hazy, foggy feeling-feelings of a mere 30,000 years ago were the seeds of mankind's greatest achievements. The mental energy that has created all these feats cannot be switched off. We can neither turn back nor stop the clock. What we have learned and what we know cannot later be unlearned and "unknown." Once we can appreciate the beauty of a perfect red rose, we cannot imagine it as a great white shark. We can, and we must, move ever forward.

But this bumbling process of growth and development was not physical. Man is not the fastest-running beast; many animals are swifter. Our endurance and agility are limited. Many creatures are more powerful than we are. Our tree-climbing ability is weak. We have no jaws or claws for attack, and no teeth or talons for defense. It could be suicidal to use our arms as wings. Our hands and feet make poor paddles. In the kingdom of the fishes, our breathing apparatus would be fatal. We cannot echo-find like bats, see in the dark like owls, follow scents like dogs, or sense vibrations like snakes. As global navigators, Arctic terns humble us. At tunneling a mole would outdo us; at burrowing we would be beaten by both Roger and Peter Rabbit.

Physically, we are puny. We are born unarmed and unprotected, yet we have colonized Earth. We command this planet and we've walked on the moon. We're actively exploring our Solar System, learning about our expanding, evolving universe and theorizing about infinity and cosmic forevers. How? What is our secret? Who are we? Or rather, *what* are we?

We are not human doings, but human beings. If we had to rely on our bodies alone we could not be effective. As doers, we would not endure. Something would fall on us, tickle us, bite us, eat us. We would have been one of millions of species swept away in evolution's survival of the fittest. No, what makes us great is something we do before we act. That something is quick, free, and devastatingly effective.

We are *Homo sapiens,* the Thinker. We think before we act—first the think and then the thing. We also have the ability to remember what we do and what happens to us, and to learn from the experience. This puts us firmly at the pinnacle of known intelligent life. It makes us *Homo sapiens sapiens:* the Wise Ones.

We are born physically defenseless; our mind is our only weapon. The essence of being human is mind. Mind is supreme. With memory, thought and emotion, and imagination, we have not just survived, but also thrived. These are the paramount aspects of mind.

And remember: Memory is the heart of mind.

5

May I Pick Your Brain?

What is all this talk of brain and mind, thoughts and ideas, feeling and emotion? What does it mean? How does it affect you? Why should you try to understand it? It seems too complicated and difficult to make any sense. And what has all this got to do with memory, anyway? Is this what you are asking yourself? If you are, that's good. We're on our way.

Others might not think as you do, but they would still have a choice. In an extreme case, they could remain passive, pour another drink, and go back to watching TV. They will spend the rest of their days asking, wistfully, why their life never improves. Or, heaven forbid, they will expect tomorrow to be a little worse than today. Alternatively, they could be like you: consciously continuing to grow and develop, and staying excited at the prospect of changing for the better.

Let *Yumm* cause an uprising within you—one that is internal and mental. Use this *little red book* to carry on your own process of self-replenishment and improvement.

You are probably asking questions; in other words, you are fruitfully involved in *Yumm*. You may doubt your ability ("Will I be able to understand this stuff"?), but press on; universal truths are simple to grasp. You want to know and to learn. Curiosity—the desire to know—means that you are functioning at the very highest level.

The brain is a physical thing. You could plop it on the slab in the kitchen, chop it up, and feed it to DiggedyDog. The value of your brain does not lie in what it is, but in what it does: process information.

But to describe the brain as a data processor is about as helpful as saying that the Sun is hot. Both statements are true, but they aren't very useful. Yet it is the heat radiating from the Sun that makes possible that vital energy called life. Without the Sun, life could not be; without a brain, you could not be. The Sun is to the world what your brain is to your being. The Sun is the source. It nurtures life, growth, and rebirth. Your brain is your fountainhead, the wellspring of your functioning.

The amount of data that our brains process is truly humungous. So vast and varied is the brain's capacity that only in the last twenty or thirty years have we developed sufficiently to become aware of what it does. So huge is the range of products and processes of the brain that we are only just beginning to unfold its myriad mysteries and secrets. Only now are we awakening to its endless possibilities. The building blocks for all these processes are stored pieces of information. And the word we use for this fundamental material that is stored away for ongoing use is…memory.

From the point at which our earliest ancestors started to appear, between two and four million years ago, the brain has continuously evolved. In fact, we have not one but three major systems between our ears.

The oldest part sits at the base of the brain and is called the brain stem. It controls the fundamental life functions such as body temperature, heart rate, and blood pressure, and it regulates our basic biochemistry. This early brain, which we have in common with much less-evolved species such as crocodiles, is concerned with the complex processes of keeping life going. Although vital life support is of some importance to us, it is not the focus of the capabilities we consider to be mind.

On top of this reptilian mechanism for maintaining life is the second part of the brain: a group of interconnected structures called the limbic system, which presided over our passage from sea-dwelling to land-living animals. The limbic system (from the Greek *limbus*, meaning threshold) reached its present state of development about two hundred million years ago and differs from its more primitive ancestor in its basic structure, in appearance, and in the kind of activity by which it is driven.

Life began in water because water is stable, and hence a less-threatening environment. Over many ages, water creatures became amphibious and eventually developed into land dwellers. In order to live on land they had to evolve a more complex brain, for life in a world of water is very different from life in a universe of air.

The dangers faced on dry land and from the air are far greater than those found in water. A different set of challenges faced the new order. Weight and temperature had to be regulated, water and thirst handled in new ways, the breathing system redesigned, the demands of a radically new diet met, and movement completely redefined. But these were essentially technical and mechanical concerns in a changed world of things.

To meet the new threats, another dimension was needed. This new capacity was not to be found in the physical domain of longer claws or stronger jaws. Mere bodily adaptations were not enough for significant development. Something more advanced had to grope its way into existence. The huge leap came from within the creature itself. From a formless, invisible inner world emerged the added dimension of *feeling*. Over the millennia, as terrain and climate changed and changed again, our range of sensitivity expanded and intensified.

Over time, we became creatures of emotion. Emotions are reactions to the things, events, and people of everyday life. We experience them as sensations that can be mighty forces. They are a vital part of us today, much as they were with Theghn and his remote ancestors. Emotions are critical to our functioning because they act as a kind of in-house priority system. They give value to life by separating the important from the not-so-important. They are potent allies and efficient servants; if not disciplined and controlled, they can make diabolical masters. Emotions inspire action. In fact, emotions underpin all our actions.

In the realm of bodily form and physical matter, they influence processes such as pulse rate and rate of breathing. In the kingdom of the mental, at the level of the psyche, emotions work on our states of mind, dictating excitement or calmness, intense joy or hopeless despair. They determine our moods as we roller-coaster from one feeling to another, and this impacts everything that we do.

We have a name for the sum of all our actions—*behavior*. Supporting all our behavior is our knowledge of what has gone before. We have a word for that as well—*memory*.

Will, determination, and logic are useful allies. But the ultimate natural partner for an effective memory is emotion. If, within an organized framework and using the right tools and techniques, you can feel what you choose to remember at an elementary, gut level, you can know that you know. That sort of primary, knowing-that-you-know makes information unforgettable!

Yumm will provide both an organized framework and a network of simple, easy-to-use tools and techniques so that you can start to gently cultivate the infinite possibilities of your unlimited, magnificent memory. Your instinctive creativity will be nurtured and developed, your inborn inventiveness will not be able to hide any longer, and your innate ingenuity will be encouraged and welcomed as a vital part of the remembering process. Your natural ability to innovate has a pivotal role to play; imagination—your most powerful asset—will be expanded, and so will your whole appreciation of life.

With deeper understanding, appropriate structures, and the correct tools, practice is more efficient and hence more effective. That adds up to confidence. And that's fun.

> You have embarked on
> an endless and exciting voyage:
> the sublime adventure into
> the universal,
> the mighty…
> your mind.
> I salute you.

6

Umm...Just a Thought

The cortex was the last of the three major brain systems to evolve. Ago and Theghn, a paltry 30,000 years back, were teetering on the brink of a discovery that was to lead to a vastly expanded and vibrant world of reasoning, under-standing, and thinking. Our ancestors were developing mental tools that would allow them to claw themselves out of the rut of primitive ignorance. The effects of those evolutionary revelations were to be profound and tumultuous.

The cerebral cortex looks like a cabbage that covers the rest of the brain, and it is folded so that it can fit within the small human head. But this unattractive addition to the brain is the ultimate triumph. For it is in this outer layer that we solve problems, make decisions, and choose to take risks. It is here that you will use *r*eason to *u*nderstand and *t*hink about memory. So it is here that you will *rut* about *Yumm*.

By the way, my Collins dictionary tells me that a *rut* is an annually recurrent period of sexual excitement in certain male cud-chewers.

It tells me further that to be in a *rut* is to be caught in dreary or unchanging routine.

If you are in a rut; you can use the thinking presented in this book to improve your memory and thereby broaden your horizons, and start to clamber toward a more meaningful life. As you continue to link all your uniquely human facets of mind, you will create bold new forms of yourself.

You will become more *you*, and will build for yourself a life that is fuller, richer, and bigger.

Life is based largely on seeking comfort and avoiding pain. Man is a pleasure-seeking organism, actively seeking out that which gives him joy. We are attracted to happiness. However, we get bored easily. Yesterday's stimulation may be uninteresting today and effectively forgotten tomorrow. So our constant search for the balance between stimulus and contentment is an ongoing process of progress, growth, and change; of striving to expand and unfold; of becoming more aware and more conscious. For you and me, the whole process of living seems to be no more than a steady and slow unrolling of consciousness of what goes on around us.

The rock that both Theghn and Naauw sat astride is a frenzy of molecules. So are you and I. But that boulder could not feel "sat astride." It has no life, and so no consciousness. However, a plant is aware of the conditions of the soil, temperature, and humidity. A perfect red rose will bloom in spring, but its awareness is very limited. Fishes, when compared with plants and vegetables, have more advanced levels of awareness. A great white shark will be aware of water temperature, food availability, danger, and mating urges, but little more. DiggedyDog will form deep and trusting relationships with her pups and at least one human. She functions on an even higher level of awareness.

And then there is you—and the rest of the human race. You have the ultimate awareness: consciousness, which is the ability to think about your own mental processes. You can sit and ponder, and know...and know that you know. This is the reason why you have dominion over rocks and roses, sharks and dogs. You can be deliberately aware of *you*—your moods, feelings, thoughts, prejudices, and preferences. This self-consciousness gives you the power to choose intentionally.

Your life is a never-ending torrent of choices. You can choose to function at lower levels of consciousness, simply existing and unthinkingly imitating the bliss of the cabbage. You can choose to do nothing more than hoard and protect your possessions, eat, drink, shag, and shut-eye, floating like a day-old turd in a toxic tank. Or you can soar to higher levels of consciousness, allowing yourself to transcend imagined limitations.

You can create for yourself an infinitely rich internal universe that will determine what you think about yourself and the external world. This will establish the way you act. In other words, the way you feel about yourself, down to the very deepest levels, will dictate your behavior. So your internal, private domain creates your external, public behavior. This inner realm is called "mind," and it is made up of thoughts.

It is a great misfortune that we do not have an efficient mechanism for isolating thoughts when we want to, for they must surely be a finer, higher form of energy. Ideally, we should be able to pin them down and examine them, because they are blueprints for possible action. But only when soaked in emotion do ideas become compelling. Thoughts and ideas, saturated with feeling, impel action.

Thoughts and feelings are elusive, slippery little things that are invisible, without form and lacking dimension. You can't go to the supermarket and buy a measure of free will, or a bundle of emotion. Feelings can't be bottled; you can't add a pinch of choice to your supper. These are not things. They are concepts; they have no existence in the world of matter. Because they have no substance, you cannot see or touch them. A measure of freedom can never be bartered for a burden of guilt or a cover of confusion. You could never buy $10 worth of fear, faith, or forgiveness. All the reserves of Japan Inc. could not purchase one iota of either blame or courage. A Russian ruble can be no exchange for a rushin' rage.

Thoughts that are strung together for a purpose are called thinking; thinking is, indeed, a thin king. (Of course, it is possible to allow others to control some or all of your thinking. In that case you would be permitting another person to direct a part—or the whole—of your future.) Recently you have trapped some thinking. The gossamer energy that is an idea attracted feeling. Combined with emotion, that thought grabbed your attention. So you did some further thinking, and then you used your uniquely human attribute of free will. You decided to act, and so you are reading these words right now. The decision to do something was a thought. The thought caused the action.

All behavior is learned, and most is automatic and repetitive. It became automatic through acts done over and over again. This mindless repetition is called habit. Habit is like being on automatic pilot. It frees us to get on with new, possibly more important and challenging stuff. At different times in our lives, we have all had to learn to walk, to contemplate the importance of memory, and to scratch our noses. Now we can do all three at the same time, without even being conscious of what we are doing.

But habit can be a negative influence. Are some of your everyday beliefs out-dated? How much of your automatic behavior weakens you? Is some of your thinking about memory archaic? How many of your actions that involve remembering debase you? Could your attitude toward recalling and recollecting be based on plain ignorance because of…because of a failure to rethink?

Look again. Now is the time to review this thinking. Be honest about yourself. Be honest *with* yourself. It takes some focused, and often frustrating, thought (supported by practice) to produce deep-seated learning. *Yumm* is designed to empower you with appropriate thinking for effective memory.

I hope that *Yumm* has already started you reconsidering. But your desire to improve and learn more about your memory is merely your thought on this topic. Your determination to succeed is merely your thought of doing so. The idea of success is just the thought of success. Your relationship to everything and everybody in your life is nothing more than thought.

Your body is designed to move, and this movement is the work of muscles. But muscles cannot move by themselves. Without a thought to activate them, they are idle. Muscles can only expand or contract—opposite versions of the same movement. This taut or that relaxed position occurs in response to a signal, and that comes from a thought. Without an idea to guide it, a muscle has nothing to do. It cannot inspire itself to action, just as breakfast cannot prepare itself.

Everything that has happened to you before this instant is called your past. You cannot go back to what you actually experienced five minutes, five hours, five days, or five anythings ago. You can't turn "now" back. You are not able to phys-ically relive yesterday's romance, but you can in another way. How? In your mind. What you re-create will be a feat of memory and imagination. And that can only be a mental event, pure thought, an affair to remember…

Similarly, all that will happen to you *after* this precise moment is your future. That is what future means: the time still to come. By using your astounding powers of imagination, which relies on memory for information, you can cre-ate a future—but only in your mind. You can imagine an amour. Surely this could only be…thought?

So if your past and your future, your memories and your expectation, are just mental processes, what about this microsecond called right now, this present moment, or this very instant? Could this also be, umm …just a thought?

You can control one aspect of your life: your thinking. Yesterday, today, and tomorrow are merely thoughts. You can control your conscious memories: green and gold, embarrassing, sweet or sour, exhilarating, big or small, inspiring…

Could they also be,
umm …just a thought?

7

Simply You and *Me*

Your world is your mind. Your mind is the core of your life. Without your mind to make sense of it, the universe wouldn't exist for you. You could not respond to the glow of a sunrise over the grasslands, the smell of woodsmoke, the sour taste of a lemon, the romance of a full moon reflected off the ocean, the touch of a loved one, or the song of a robin.

In fact, every experience of your life is a construction of your mind, an interpretation of signals arriving from elsewhere—sometimes from "in here," but mostly from "out there." Your mind, glued together by thinking and feeling, is the one thing that cannot be taken from you without your permission. It is yours for as long as you want it to be. Build your mind, and you build your life. Let it vegetate, and you'll create a cabbage.

The raw material of mind is information, or rather, that which is remembered. Some things are borne in mind consciously, but most are not. Without memory, there is no mind. So in building your memory, you are building your mind. Both mind and memory can be deliberately strengthened and developed with exercise, just as the human body is strengthened and toned through exercise in order to function more effectively.

Specific physical exercises are designed for specific muscles. In making them work, stretching and contracting, they break through old limits to new, suppler frontiers. *Yumm* will help you to work on your own mind in exactly that way: stretching and shaping your memory and extending it to more subtle fringes. By exercising and developing your memory you will become more alert, more sensitive to the present moment. You will be more mindful. In short, you will be more *you*.

Mao Zedong, the father of Chinese communism, in his *Little Red Book*, simply instructed a fifth of the world's population as to precisely what they should think and exactly how they should behave. This *little red book* is less harsh; more suggestive. I demonstrate how you might start to think in another, slightly different way, in addition to your current forms, and what you would then be able to achieve over and above your present levels. The choice is yours.

Most people choose to live in the past and ask why. A few choose to use the past, while living in the present, to create their future by asking, "Why not?"

The basic aim of *Yumm* is to help you take more active control of your thought processes and to take greater control of your future. Since you have nothing to lose, why not?

This *little red book* is designed to make you more conscious of mind and memory; to set you on an ongoing journey of gentle and easy, though effective, thinking; and to guide you along a lifelong program of mental exercise. The focus of *Yumm* is conscious memory, which is learning, which is knowledge. Conscious memory is not an island unto itself; it is an integral, vital aspect of mind. To develop memory is to enlarge and expand the whole mind.

This requires conscious and deliberate processes. I have seen it written and heard it said that knowledge is power. That is seldom true. To bring something worthwhile into being, knowledge must be converted into purposeful action; to be effective, learning must be applied; to realize a desired end, memory must be used; to achieve anything, something must be done. Action is a vital ingredient.

Memory without action is about as useful as a telephone handset would have been to Theghn and his merry men. In addition, conscious, effective memory is not the result of happenstance, fortune, or good luck. It does not work on the installment plan. There is no credit system. One can't remember well today and put in the necessary practice tomorrow. Now is cash. Cash is now.

There is an unchangeable order that has to be followed: plant first, then reap. First the think and then the thing. But the best-laid plans can be foiled by circumstances and things "out there." Not so with memory. Memory is "in here." You can have complete control over your own mental processes. Nobody else can defeat you, unless, of course, you allow them to. Only you can frustrate you.

And so to you and *me*: *m*ental *e*xercise…

Imagine a typical exercise program for fitness and general toning. You might begin with a few minutes of stretches to warm up and loosen the muscles. Then a little more intense effort, jogging on the spot to deepen breathing and increase pulse rate. While the legs are warm, a few exercises to strengthen and shape them. Another series for the neck, shoulders, and arms. Another for the torso—chest, stomach, and lower back. Over time, depending on how you feel, you take longer and work out more intensely. But you still keep to the basics. You add new exercises and work harder, but you never overlook the fundamentals on which your whole regimen relies.

In the beginning, your whole routine might have taken only ten minutes of gentle exercise. A couple of weeks later, you might be doing thirty minutes of harder work. After a couple of months, the session might be a full hour of intense, exhausting exertion. After a while, and with much effort, comes confidence: "I look better. I know it."

This commitment takes a lot of time, energy, and money. Few of us can maintain this sort of schedule for any length of time. To most of us, the eternal quest to look like an Olympic superhero just isn't a priority. And besides, it simply isn't practical to sustain such high ongoing involvement in physical fitness.

But what has four walls and a garden, and offers a huge range of exercises? Yes, your own home. What with digging, hammering, painting, polishing, scraping, sweeping, cutting, and weeding, there's not a muscle of the body untouched. Now add raking, scrubbing floors, kneading bread, cleaning a car, and grooming a pet. Lifting and carrying a baby will do plenty for your arms and shoulders. Playing with a child can be fantastic exercise. Often you leave the house to walk DiggedyDog or yourself. At work you use the stairs instead of the lift; in the shopping mall you refuse to use the escalator, and around town and the countryside, you walk. Exercise is an ongoing, permanent part of your life. You use and enjoy your body.

This is the model for memory training as well, except that you do not go out to a public place. On the contrary, you remain within yourself—in your own most intimate home. You don't need complicated techniques or high-tech equipment. There aren't any, anyway. You explore and develop that wonderful universe that is your mind. The golden rule must be "nice 'n' easy". There's no rush. You're involved in a lifelong process of growing yourself—in this instance, from the internal dimensions outward. *Yumm* and you should be an ideal partnership. This *little red book* should make you mindful of memory and how central it is to everything that you do, and everything that you are. Without memory, you simply couldn't be. Hopefully, you are already more appreciative of what it does for you.

All the tools and techniques covered from here on will enable you to gradually strengthen and expand every nook and cranny of your memory. Practice them in your mind (where else?) whenever you can. And that's one of the greatest advantages of *me:* you don't need a car, a 25th hour in each day, or winning the national lottery. All you need is to schedule—any time, any place—a bit of internal effort. A good time to do this is when your body is active, but your mind is gathering dust.

Many of us pass a significant part of the day with our minds in mothballs. We lie in bed, trying to get to sleep or waiting to get up. We lie in the bath with the gray matter just ticking over; while in the shower we mooch—mentally. We spend a great deal of our lives waiting: for a taxi, a bus, a plane, a child. We wait—in a check-out queue, at the bank, for a ticket, to see someone, or for a call to come through. Most of us spend a lot of time in transit every day, driving or being driven. And we wait—for the TV commercials to finish, for the tank to be filled, for the machine to complete its washing cycle, for the supper to cook. We all have long moments of irritation, impatience, and boredom.

At these times the body is presiding, and the mind, by default, is in limbo. Use these barren patches to stimulate yourself, to be creative and constructive. Instead of seeing such periods as wasted, you can employ them constructively. Profit from these minutes by exercising your mind. Seize these moments to learn and use the techniques, to think about memory, and to exercise the whole thinking process. Almost immediately, and with minimum effort, confidence will come: "I feel better. I love it."

Much of our life is dominated by habit, that unconscious, automatic thought that causes unconscious, automatic behavior. So many of the hours of our day are filled with mindless routine we perform automatically. We are guided by an unthinking hand that frees the mind for higher, more valuable pursuits. And this is a vital aspect of our human genius.

Can you remember anything about brushing your teeth this morning? You can brush your teeth (a physical process) and train your memory (a mental process) at the same time. The whole getting-up-in-the-morning routine is largely habit. So is getting to and from work. Turn such valuable moments to good account and benefit from *me*. Take short breaks during the day to review the tools and techniques of memory and what you have remembered. Equally important, review what you have not remembered, and why. Think about memory. Chew over what you have been able to recall. Ponder what you have forgotten. Reflect on why this should be.

Do this any time, any place—standing, sitting, lying down; while active or in mental neutral; dressed or undressed. Just do it—as much and as often as possible. Grab your unlimited, magnificent memory by the scruff of the neck. Think about memory. Practice…with *mental exercise*. Play, with *me*.

> To enrich your life,
> Extend your mind.
> To extend your mind,
> Expand your memory.
> To expand your memory…
> do *me*.
> More *me*, bigger you.
> Ho humm …it's just a thought.

8

On Turning over a New Life

Every single one of us is born with a mind. This invisible dimension came along naturally as part of the miraculous bundle called "You." Because your mind has been with you since before you can remember, you have taken it for granted. Few of us have given our mind so much as a passing glance, so we are not really conscious of our essence.

Not many of us have ever pondered, reflected on, or considered such concepts as thinking and feeling, imagination, or memory. On the rare occasions that you may have spared a thought for that magnificent faculty called "your memory," you probably abused it. That was B4. But you don't do that any more, do you?

How did you come to be reading these words? Did you happen to stumble on this book by chance, and you're just browsing through it out of idle curiosity? Was it lent to you by a friend? Are you flipping through *Yumm* in a bookstore because you feel that it might be of value to you? Or have you bought this *little red book* because you want to start improving your memory?

Whatever the reason, is it in response to a quiet whisper inside yourself, however tiny, that could be saying, "These few pages might be good for me"? I hope that is the case. I hope also that this quiet, though insistent voice is lovingly suggesting to you that you can and should develop yourself, even more than you are doing at the moment.

In a world that is changing at an ever-increasing pace, if we stand still, we fall behind. Life these days demands that we constantly learn and grow, just to keep up. Each of us has a responsibility to ourselves to consciously and deliberately enlarge our knowledge and experience. We owe it to ourselves to make our lives an active, lifelong learning adventure.

May I assume that you are reading *Yumm* because there are aspects of your memory that you would like to improve? If so, your first specific questions to yourself could be: "What aspect of my memory would I like to enhance, and why? Do I want to remember names more effectively, be better at recalling numbers, or understand why Aunt Mabel 'loses' her keys? Do I want to appreciate the real benefit of getting older, develop my mind and thinking processes, and increase my powers of observation? Would I like to expand my creative imagination, enhance my self-confidence, or amplify my consciousness so as to enrich my whole experience of life?"

All of these, none of the above, a few…which ones? Only you can decide. Begin with the end in mind: What is your purpose? What is your *intention?*

Naauw A'Daze is an amateur painter who has learned to be conscious and sensitive. While these attributes came freely, they did not come free. She could not pay for her expanded consciousness with dollars, deutschmarks, or doddle nuts. She had to pay with *attention.*

Because of her training, Naauw would probably appreciate the portrait of Mona Lisa more than the person who paints her house would. As an architect, her husband Yest can look at a building and see a thousand more technical details than her untrained eye can. He is an expert in the design of buildings because he has learned about their construction.

Similarly, an experienced seaman scanning the skies and the swells of the sea would gain far more information from watching them than the landlubber would. A paratrooper, after a stimulating day of playing war games, is deaf to a hint of mint, unfeeling to a touch of thyme. He's almost senseless.

A gourmet is highly sensitive to the flavor of food and to the mix of shape, texture, and color on the plate. A gourmand is not interested in quality; he merely fills his ample belly with quantity. So it is with the wine connoisseur who appreciates the delicacy and finesse of the winemaker's art. The wino drinks more but is oblivious to the subtleties of taste, aroma, and color, for he has an altogether different point of view.

As we focus and hone our attention, we not only experience more, but we also experience better. This inner unfolding is personal development, a lifelong process of increasing sensitivity to more and clearer impressions. And that depends upon focusing our mind and increasing our powers of attention. Woozy observations produce after their own kind: foggy little scraps that are neither here nor there—the stuff of dim and misty memories. As the mind is, so is the person: fuzzy, diffused, and ineffectual.

Keen and alert individuals, on the other hand, always have their attention on the spot, concentrated and focused. Their sense impressions are clear, vivid, and precise. They have superior mental habits and a sharper mind, and so are often a more valuable person to themselves and others. Such a person usually has an excellent memory.

Only you, and your intention to pay attention, can start to unleash your capacity to remember. You need to look and notice and observe ...*more*. You will sharpen all your senses, as well as becoming more conscious, alert, and sensitive. You will become a more active participant in this wonderful experience called life.

In pursuit of our *intention*, are you prepared to pay the price—with *attention?*

To develop any skill takes practice, and memory is no exception. Nice 'n' easy, gentle and relaxed, have fun—that's the way. With your newfound "memory-consciousness," practice will happen naturally throughout your days anyway, and it's a lifelong process. Positive results are immediate, which will encourage you to deliberately keep on remembering better. You will automatically be both *consistent* and *persistent*.

With intention will come consistent and persistent attention.

As with so much in life, there is one great Satan when it comes to good remembering. There is an opportunistic force of evil always hovering, waiting to exploit the slightest weakness or apprehension; a constant worry; an ever-present menace that snuffs out enthusiasm and quashes vitality. This vile specter cheats ideas and thoughts of their excitement and energy by mutilating doing and massacring action. This noxious presence flourishes on apathy and indifference; it loathes purposeful effort. But in the face of understanding, it disappears, for the gloom of ignorance is its hellish domain. It ceases to exist in the glow of the light, for this character is a prince of darkness—the sworn enemy of progress.

This lord of no-light is *anxiety* itself.

There is no place in the life of your memories for fear and tension.

However, easy remembering is its own natural antidote. Toxic thinking such as "I won't remember" is devoured by effortless recall. Old, outdated beliefs along the lines of "My memory is no good" carry no weight in the face of instant recollection. Effective memory castrates fear and neuters tension.

I hope you have already come to understand that any statement similar to "I can't remember" is a lie—an insult to your essence, an outrage to your soul—because your magnificent memory is inherently limitless. You can remember anything, if you want to.

Simply trust your memory …your mind …yourself.

9

Peat, Peat, and More Peat

Peat is a substance rather like moist cake, formed from peat moss that accumulated over thousands of years. Peat lands are swamps, marshes, or bogs. The words are often used interchangeably to describe wetlands, but strictly speaking they refer to very different ecosystems. Swamps are dominated by trees, marshes by grasses, and bogs by mosses, heaths, and rushes.

Millions of years ago, there were great forests of huge trees whose only modern relatives are the meager little growths that we call mosses. As these trees and their undergrowth died, they fell back into the water-saturated soil in which they grew. Over the eons, through physical and chemical processes, this soggy mush called peat was changed into coal. So the formation of peat is the first stage in the transformation of vegetation into a rock that burns. Even today, coal is still the main source of power for heat and light worldwide.

Four to six thousand years ago, bogs covered much of northern Europe. People lived on the high ground and farmed in the lowlands. Those eerie moonscapes of misty mosses that gave way underfoot were the uninhabited parts of the countryside, for they could only be crossed by certain paths. These bogs have always haunted us. Men and women regarded them with suspicion and fear, so they came to be viewed as sacred sites associated with the gods and the afterlife.

From time to time, human sacrifices were thrown into the bogs to appease the supernatural powers. Because of their high acidity, wetness, low temperature, and absence of oxygen, the bogs preserved the bodies instead of decaying them. Thus the bogs of northern Europe, where some 2,000 bodies have been discovered, became a repository of the past—a sinister burial ground containing many clues to the life of these ancient wetland dwellers.

Across the Atlantic Ocean, the dead of an early American Indian society lay under an ever-deepening shroud of peat for more than 7,000 years. Tenderly buried in a shallow pond in central Florida, these people were hunter-gatherers who made seasonal rounds throughout the region that is known today for Walt Disney World and the Kennedy Space Center. Their bones and artifacts speak poignantly of a little-understood culture and reveal levels of craft previously undocumented in the New World during that era.

What's all this about peat, peat, and more peat?
Well, the word occurs more than once,
so it is a re-peat.
And
RE-PETITION
RE-PETITION
RE-PETITION
RE-PETITION
RE-PETITION
RE-PETITION
RE-PETITION
RE-PETITION
RE-PETITION
RE-PETITION
RE-PETITION
RE-PETITION
is essential to effective re-calling, re-collecting, and
re-membering.

By the way, in his dictionary, Mr. Collins tells me that a *petition* is a request to a higher authority. In this case, could the higher authority be mind…and memory?

PART TWO
A Bird's-Eye View—
The Six GUTs of Memory

10

Once More, with Feeling

The brain is a continuously evolving organism. It is a living, vibrant thing. Today it is a celebration of many hundreds of millions of years of growth and development in response to constant menace and ever-present danger. Brain's highest function is mind—a steady unfolding and expanding of consciousness. I hope that you will make *Yumm* a part of this flow. But remember that this consciousness is not found in any other life form. This "I know, and I know that I know" is unique to you and me and all our kind.

The genesis of mind lay in the slow and ponderous awakening of sensitivity and feeling. A couple of hundred million years ago, our ancestors were staggering down the path toward emotion, a route that would cause us to be creatures of the vilest cruelty and hate, on one hand, and of the most tender compassion and love on the other.

Mind in its present, potentially limitless form is a phenomenon that has existed for only a few tens of thousands of years. A trifling 30,000 years ago, Theghn and his men had no sophisticated language. They had no effective method of transferring ideas and thoughts—they were mindless. Without language, they were unable to think properly.

Stop reading for a couple of minutes. Try to imagine what your life would be like without language. It is literally unthinkable, isn't it?

So your mind and mine are the most recent and tiniest tick in the whole vast tick-tock of time. But the effect is breathtaking. Our minds enable us to master and manipulate our world to the extent that we do. While it may not justify our behavior, our possession of a (conscious) mind does explain our dominance.

Evolution—the progressive development to more and more complex forms of life—does not have a grand plan. Nature has no master strategy. If you and I are sufficiently in sync with our environment at this moment, we'll survive. If not, we must adapt...quickly. Nature has no favorites. An adaptation that works should make it through to another day. So mind is a syndicate of systems and circuits; a blend of the primitive and the progressive; a mix of thoughts and feelings, ideas and emotions.

What are thoughts and ideas? They are cold and sterile little bits of energy, dry data that are the basis of hard fact. A thought might be of a shark, great and white. Or a flower, a rose in fact—its color deep red, its smell strong, its thorns sharp. Thoughts and ideas do not inspire action.

What are feelings and emotions? Feelings interpret and give meaning to thoughts and ideas and cause us to act or react. In your mind's eye, see that great white shark. Imagine your friend thrashing and screaming in helpless agony. He is drowning in a bubbling sea of his own blood, attacked while surfing in the waves off the beach. You might feel your flesh crawling and tingling each time you relive (in your mind, where else?) the memory of that morbid affair.

Add feeling and emotion to that deep-red rose and it takes on a whole new significance. It might express your adoration for another person. When you actually give the rose to that person, you experience an outpouring of tenderness, caring, and love. Later, memories of that same experience cause the same sort of emotions to affect you again.

Emotions and feelings can be immensely powerful. Mind is a continuous interaction between its own different facets—an endless interchange of ideas and feelings, thoughts and emotions. In order to make the mind more effective, some sort of consistent structure must be established.

This is what culture is all about. The old want to pass on the best to the young, imprinting the next generation with the values and standards that their family and their wider community see as desirable. From our culture, we learn who we are and what is expected of us. Education builds on the foundation of family by imparting knowledge to minds that are fertile and prepared to receive it. Experience—what we might call lived knowledge—should expand and enrich our lives. All this should create a growing body of accumulating wisdom—the ongoing ability to be of increasing value to oneself, and then to be of greater value to others.

All this personal development rests on the bedrock of memory. Just like every-thing else, memory demands method, organization, and system to be effective. But this framework of order must not be unbending and inflexible. Quite the contrary, it should be free-wheeling, fun, and flexible, for it is merely a set of guidelines, a frame of reference.

Nothing is fixed and rigid. In fact, the essence of memory improvement is that thinking and feeling are a gentle, flowing partnership. Ideas and emotion merge in pervasive cooperation:

rut, with *me.*

11

Patched Parachute or
Nifty Network?

And so I come to the first of the six Great Universal Truths: the GUTs of memory.

A GUT is a cosmic law, fixed and unchangeable, like gravity. It is a principle of the natural order of things, not a creation of Man. GUTs are fundamental; they can be neither created nor altered. Work against a GUT, and you will fail; work with one, and you might succeed. Let a perfect red rose drop from your hand and it will fall downward, every time and anywhere. It will not skid sideways one time in eleven or rise upward on every seventh drop.

There is order throughout the universe. Even our little nook in the cosmic forever is a unified whole, *a* system—*the* Solar System. In the same way, there must be order in our lives and in our thinking. Memory is no exception. To be effective, our memory must be organized. The closer we align ourselves with the GUTs of memory, the better we will remember.

With *Yumm,* you have made yourself aware of memory and its awesome importance in your life. Soon, very soon, you will begin to believe in your capacity to recognize and recall virtually anything you choose. With experience, you will develop both a positive belief in and a confident expectation of your memory. This *little red book* will give you a knowledge of memory methods and systems, of tools and techniques. They are all natural and fun, and very, very effective.

Favorable "habits of thought"—or "attitudes," as they are often called—will emerge as surely as day follows night. The only way to end the darkness of the night is to introduce the glow of the light. So you must start by looking in the right place for illumination—not outside at the lights, but inside at enlightenment. This is the ongoing process of unrolling understanding that I call U2, or *You too.* You will be changing more of the virtual you into the real you.

You have infinite capability, unlimited capacity, and endless potential. You are pure possibility. By setting out to improve your ability to remember, you will be developing more of you. You will be acting deliberately, with intention.

Play with words and have fun with ideas; your imagination is childish and childlike. Bring joy to your very soul…travel in time, visit cyberspace, levitate, gravitate, whiz, zoom. Be in awe, be grateful. Propel yourself out of the reason/understand/think mode: the *rut.* Stimulate, challenge, and extend your creativity, your thinking process, and your mind.

Thoughts are the food of mind. Memories are the building blocks, the protein of thoughts. Without memory there is, well, *nothing*, and nothing comes from nothing. If the cupboard is bare, there ain't no supper. Talking of food reminds me…

Your kitchen is organized. It is unlikely that you'll have the garden tools in the dry goods cupboard, or wrenches and car grease with the cups and saucers. Pots and pans are no doubt together in one section, with appliances kept somewhere else. While the blender may be in a cupboard, the toaster is probably conveniently on a work surface near the bread box. Herbs and spices are all racked side by side with the labels clearly visible. The meat for dinner is in the refrigerator; the fish caught the previous weekend is in the freezer.

The vitamin-enriched, mineral-enhanced, energy-boosted, turbo-charged, steak-'n'-strawberry hyper-chunks for DiggedyDog are under the sink. If he wants a shoe to chew, he knows the bedroom is the most likely place to find one. Even in his small universe there is a basic order.

Imagine that you intend to make the hole of a doughnut. You know that you will find the recipe at the library, but when you get there every single last book has been thrown into an enormous pile in the parking lot. All the information is still there and available, but it is not accessible. Disappointed, you head for home. Disaster awaits you: Aunt Mabel has run amok. She's trashed your kitchen, and everything's in a heap on the floor. She's even locked Diggedy in the tool shed.

In both the library and your kitchen, the same thing has happened: *chaos, disorder, mess.* Look at the words in the previous paragraph: *thrown, pile, disappointed, disaster, run amok, trashed, heap,* and so on. In this context, they are all negative, denying words. Remember how hamstrung Theghn was without words and the power of speech? They express our thinking, both to others and to ourselves. The words listed above are words associated with loss and limitation, all because of a lack of system and method.

"Your world is your mind. Your mind is the essential core of your life. Without your mind to make sense of it, the world wouldn't exist for you. You would not respond to the glow of a sunrise over the grasslands, the smell of wood smoke..." Do those words ring a bell?

"The raw material of mind is information, or rather, that which is remembered. Some things are borne in mind consciously, but most are not. Without memory, there is no mind." Have you read this anywhere before?

"There is order throughout the universe." Familiar?

What if the title of this book were nmMmMnn ytYlftirirdgaeo eceiiouU? Is it meaningful? Would you remember it easily? *Your Unlimited Magnificent Memory* makes more sense, doesn't it?

Would you make any sense of *Yumm* if the lines were haphazard? For example: "She experiences more than boring, uninteresting, and unmemorable. There's a tiny little senses. We must increase the delicacy of the senses so that the neck, shoulders and arms. Another for the torso."

Imagine if the pages of this *little red book* weren't in numerical order, but just printed at random: page 10 followed by page 23, or 59, or xvi...

How could the book be of value if the chapters were not systematically arranged, but instead were willy-nilly, hit or miss, aimless, left to chance, purposeless, disorganized?

Yet how many of us just drift aimlessly in regard to something as vital as memory?

The first Great Universal Truth: Memory, to be effective, needs systems. Information that we want to remember must be organized. Our potentially vast capacity for recall, like anything else, should be methodical.

GUT 1: Effective memory demands *structure.*

Oh, that reminds me: Did anybody let Diggedy out of the tool shed?

12

The Oh-Zone

Let's imagine that you and I meet. We say, "Hi." After a few seconds of silence, I say to you, "Little," and then keep quiet. You would, no doubt, be confused and reply with something like, "Little what?" You would try to find out if "little" is a question, a statement, or an observation. To what or to whom am I referring? There just isn't enough information in the single word "little," spoken out of the blue, for you to make any sense of it. It has no context, no reference points.

But what if I say "*little red book*," and then keep quiet? *Yumm* would spring to mind at once. The actual words *little, red,* and *book* are just that: words. They bear no resemblance whatsoever to the object you are holding and reading at this very moment. You have learned to associate "*little*" with size: smaller than big, but larger than tiny. "*Red*" is what we call a color, such as russet, rufous, and ruby. We have learned these meanings; we were not born with the knowledge. Such learning has been reinforced by repetition, and all of it is remembered.

Now we are both thinking of *Yumm*. Before we can communicate, we have to align our thinking—to get on the same general wavelength. To some extent each of us has to know where the other is standing—mentally, of course. At this stage, you will probably be looking for more information. So you might ask, "What about *Yumm?*" I might reply, "Have you read it? Is it interesting, valid, valuable, useful?"

You need to respond to my question so that our chat can continue, so you offer a reply: "Yes, I am reading *Yumm* at the moment, and yes, it certainly is interesting, valid…" You are getting a clearer grasp of my thinking. Often our talking is a process in which we fine-tune our own thinking. But it is also very important that in every conversation we understand what the other means.

Just as two people develop connections, so do concepts within your mind need to be associated with one another. Had you said "little" to yourself and focused on that word, your mind would have looked for further information to make sense of that blob of data. "Little" had to be linked with something else before it meant anything. "Little" cannot exist alone. Nothing can exist alone.

Why not pause right now? Bring "little" to mind. Focus on it. Relax and let your mind run free…

Now you can continue by doing what no other creature is capable of: you can deliberately analyze what happened. You are able to think about thinking, to know that you know. You can choose to be conscious.

Where did you go? Amazing, isn't it? Your mind leapt from place to person, time to space, place to space; from here to eternity, back and there—then or now, Naauw and them; from here to her and to it, theme to they or thus, all over everywhere anytime timeless or no time…no boundaries, no bounds; no limitations—no logic; no rhyme and no reason.

Mind and memory work on the principle of linking—the connecting of one thought with another. Deliberately linked thoughts equal thinking. Many of us spend most of our time just letting our thoughts drift aimlessly, uncontrolled and directionless. This lowest level of conscious mental activity is called daydreaming.

It is nearly mindless, rather like a raft without either sail or rudder. Afloat, such a raft might be useful for a seagull to perch on. But a seagull has work to do; after a while it too would move on. Usually daydreaming is like that raft, passive and ineffective—temporary, even for the birds.

We all have thoughts or feelings that are triggered by something that seems to be totally unrelated, for instance: I see a blue coat. I possibly associate the color blue with a blue mood, and not feeling well. That leads my thinking to "Oh, that reminds me, Aunt Mabel is sick."

I am nervous before a presentation: I think of a great white shark.

A perfect red rose might evoke an overwhelming feeling of tender caring for another, or a totally different thought: "Oh, that reminds me, I must feed the fish!"

"Oh, that reminds me" can be triggered by a place, time, sound, smell, memory—whatever. [Imagine that while you are waiting for the kettle to boil, you decide to hang up your jeans. When you get to the bedroom, you have "forgotten" why you went there. Go back to the kitchen, and try to recreate your previous situation. Get yourself back into the same context. The association that led you to the original thought—to hang up those denims—will probably come back to you.]

Every bit of data is joined and associated, connected and coupled, with another bit. New information (the unknown) is linked to old information (the known). As the unknown becomes the known, so mind and memory grow. A central principle of mind extension, of memory expansion, is the purposeful linking-up of the old information you already know with the new information that you intend to remember.

Both mind and memory can be seen as a three-dimensional net, with the knots representing individual thoughts and ideas, and the strings standing for the associations. No thought is isolated or stands alone. Everything must be joined to something else with knots or ties. These connections are like threads attached to the idea (*links* in Internet-speak). When we want a particular idea, we must pull the right string. If it has two strings, we double the chance of finding it. If there were twenty strings attached to the thought, we would have a much greater likelihood of finding an effective one to pull.

So the more connections and associations we make, the greater the probability of tracking down the information we want. If we link our thoughts in an organized way, we further increase the odds of being able to bring to mind what we want, when we want it. A magnificent memory cannot be built on wishing and hoping. Instead, you and your memory are an active and ongoing process deliberately enlarging the whole, huge labyrinth of mind.

The feeling of "Oh, that reminds me" I have called the Oh-Zone. This is the second of the Great Universal Truths of memory. The bedrock of an effective person is a well-organized mind. This is based in the systematic (GUT 1) linking (GUT 2) of information.

GUT 2: Effective memory is a vast network: *organize* and *link.*

Let me summarize the first two GUTs:
Organize and link…
Link and Organize…and you will find.
Link and Organize:
LO and behold!

13

You & Me R 1

Let's do an easy *mental exercise* (*me*) to illustrate the principle of linking ideas.

I am going to ask you to remember ten objects in order. You do this by making a simple and clear-cut mental picture of the first item, and the second. Then, in your mind's eye, link the images. Make a simple, clear-cut image of the third item and link it with the second. You continue like this, forming visual connections between the second and third things, then between the third and fourth, and so on.

Do not make a story, as this might lead to confusion when you retell it to yourself. Nor should you link each item to every other one so as to remember all ten. The list must be in order. To form a network is wrong. You need to create a chain—a daisy chain—connecting the articles one at a time, in sequence.

Think of a **sauce**: the liquid that you put on food to enhance its flavor. What have you got in mind: exotic **sauce** to be used as a dip for expensive seafood, or thick goo to be globbed over Killer Krumpets? Is this **sauce** smooth or lumpy, watery or creamy, glossy or without luster? What color is it?

It is vital to form an image that you can call up easily and recognize instantly as sauce every time you so choose. You might take a few seconds to form that picture, but there's no hurry. Once you have that image, stick with it.

Now bring a picture of a **seat** to mind. Do you see somebody's rump, or your favorite perch, or your Grandfather's best-loved rocking chair?

Have the **sauce** interact with the **seat**; link the two. Try to make this association as bold and vivid as possible. Be crude, funny, absurd, way-out, over the top, ridiculous, blasphemous, wacky, childlike—but be effective. Make it so that you can call up these two linked images whenever you want to, without any doubt whatsoever.

Are the two linked in your mind's eye? Did you see the two images really joined, if only for a millisecond?

Here is the list of ten things to be linked in sequence:

sauce
seat
sun
seam
sore
seal
sash
sock
safe
soap

This is the first purposeful *me*. Relax, take it easy.

Make sure you actually see both items connected, if only for a split second.

The ten items on this list are handpicked. They will serve as a framework for much of your remembering.

Please put *Yumm* down and try to recall the list.

Your recollection should be 100 percent accurate, provided that the pictures of the objects were simple and sharp, and their interaction strong.

Are you amazed at what you have remembered?

If you could not recall the chain, it could only be because the images were not clear and plain, or the associations were not intense enough. In other words, either likeness or linking wasn't powerful enough to leave a lasting impression. A chain is only as strong as its weakest link. In memory terms, your weakest link just wasn't memorable.

How well did you remember the list? Are you surprised at how much you recollected? Maybe you couldn't recall what came after, say, **sash**? How was your picture of a **sash** and of a **sock**? Was the connection weak? Free your imagination: Why not have a **sash** being worn proudly by a **sock**? If there was another weakness, where was it? Be active and question yourself; analyze, enquire, think...

Memory is a mental process, and the most important and fundamental aspect of mind. A magnificent memory is a choice—your choice.

Conscious memory, like your life, should be an active, organized, ongoing and deliberate celebration.

14

How Do You Present the Present?

We receive most of our impressions from the world "out there" via one or more of five senses. These are:

Hear here
The Big See
A Taste, bud?
The Touch-type
and
The Nose knows

Through a continuous program of training—of *me*—we hone and refine these data-gathering systems. As we develop our powers, our senses learn to receive more stimuli. They also increase in sensitivity. We amplify the delicacy of the senses so that they become more and more precise; in turn, they tune in to and pick up ever-flimsier signals. As we literally fine-tune our receivers, they become more and more acute; we make finer and finer alterations. Each stage in the process supports and encourages the others, and so the process of increasing consciousness continues. And we also pay more. We pay with more…attention.

But only meaningless pulses actually reach us from "out there." This raw data is fed to the brain to be interpreted, and to the mind to become meaningful. Only then does that "over there" become a thing with four legs. It is an elephant, not a table or a pylon. Certainly we could never recognize it as a great white shark or a perfect red rose.

Sensory input of any kind can be remembered. Until now, most of your remembering has been a hit-or-miss affair. Why? Because you were not conscious of memory. You never thought about, reflected on, or considered memory. Calling information back to mind was an imprecise, random affair. Remembering was haphazard, passive, without deliberate purpose, lacking intention.

You remembered the first list of ten items using *systems* (**GUT 1**) and *linking* ideas (**GUT 2**).

Now I am going to give you another ten objects to remember:

hose
hat
hen
home
hair
hill
hedge
hook
hive
hoop

Most of our experience of the world is put together from the information we gather through our five senses. However, each individual uses and relies on each sense to a different extent.

An artist is very visually oriented and, like Naauw, develops his consciousness and appreciation of color until he is able to detect different shades that are not obvious to most of us. He also fine-tunes his appreciation of shape and texture and how different forms combine within a composition. Remember the sailor and the soldier?

With practice and repetition, the pianist trains her appreciation of sounds and the precision of her touch to a very high degree. As she gets to know more about tone, and as her sense of feeling through her fingertips becomes more acute, her memory for both sounds and touch is refined. Each supports and invigorates the other. The hearing of a practiced musician tells her a thousand things of which the untrained person is unconscious. Likewise for the lovers of food and wine?

Maybe you are not an artist or a musician. You do have a favorite sense, though. For most of us with reasonable vision, it'll undoubtedly be your eyesight. Apparently, some 80 percent of what we learn comes through our eyes and another 10 percent or so via our ears, with the balance from our other senses—mainly touch.

Television is so powerful because of all the movement and color—the action. The visual aspect is intense. TV is also strong on sound, so it is a medium that involves two of our three most active and powerful senses: "the Big See" and "Hear here." Little wonder it grabs our emotions so strongly. The third sense is "the Touch-type."

These three vehicles can speed us to unlimited remembering, endless creative imagination, and highly effective thinking. Use these three senses for supersonic travel to a vibrant mind…sight, sound, and touch…SST. But what about "a Taste, bud?" and "the Nose knows"?

Now let's slow down and go within. Are you calm and relaxed?

Good. Gently recall both lists. In order to remember those items, which sense did you rely on most—your mind's eye? your mind's ear? Is one sense unquestionably dominant? How were the others? Did you use touch at all? Now that you are focusing on it, were there any senses that you did not use? What about taste and smell? Think about those that you didn't use.

You could develop them, couldn't you?

Since we are all stronger in some areas than we are in others, you should discover your own individual strengths and weaknesses. Do you favor your sense of hearing, sight, touch, taste, or smell? We naturally tend to work with our strong points and improve them, but they will look after themselves. Weaker areas tend to suffer more from neglect. Work with these to improve them. Train each of your senses separately, and then gradually combine them. You are looking to enhance your whole brain, your entire thinking process.

As children we lived in a world dominated by things we could see. We relied largely on images or pictures in our minds to cope with life and to play. Imagination and the mind's eye were well developed. We naturally created mental pictures. As we grew older and learned language skills, we learned to think. Our world became less thing-centered and more idea-based. "Out there" became progressively less concrete and more conceptual. We became competent at thinking in the abstract.

Formal education favors logic and reason. This approach is highly sophisticated, for we have to learn to think in words and their meanings. As you read these words, you are extracting meaning; you are not changing these words into pictures. (Just try to make sense out of this paragraph by picturing its meaning. You'll find that you can't, because it's about ideas, not objects—thinks, not things.) When words as a group, as a sentence, or as a paragraph have a message in themselves, you have to understand them by thinking in the abstract.

As we grew older, we used our ability to see in the mind's eye less and less. Often that ability was actively discouraged by adults. We were admonished with "Get your head out of the clouds!" and "Keep your feet on the ground!" As time passed, many of us lost most of that rich and splendid ability. A large part of our natural imagination was discouraged and suppressed, and it became dormant. A muscle atrophies from lack of use. For the same reason, our ability to picture in mind diminishes.

Unconsciously, we allowed ourselves to be restricted. We sort of accepted that intellect and reason were supreme and sufficient. Intuition and sensations, feelings, and emotions were seen as unfocused and undesirable, viewed almost as displaying weakness. So we tuned them out and buried them, as best we could. We even took a dim view of our own dreams and aspirations, because they were looked upon as unrealistic and impractical.

Isn't this strange? Isn't this sad?

Look again at the words I have just used: *seen, unfocused, viewed, displaying, a dim view, looked upon.* These are words and ideas expressed in the language of our eyes. They are all borrowed from our dominant sense: the Big See.

Mental picturing is a vital aspect of mind, and it is essential to your unlimited, magnificent memory. Yet this natural ability was considered to have little value! Such believing is negative, unacceptable, and counter-productive. To devalue mind is to undervalue life. Mind makes us uniquely human and unrivalled as a species. Imagination, thinking and feeling, and memory are the three pillars of mind. Your intention must be to pay attention and revitalize your creativity. You can revive your creativity by practicing little by little, in the course of each day. The Sound System is a heaven-sent launch vehicle for this effort.

So far, you have learned two lists of ten objects each. Can you bring these twenty items back to mind at will, in sequence? Here they are again:

sauce	hose
seat	hat
sun	hen
seam	home
sore	hair
seal	hill
sash	hedge
sock	hook
safe	hive
soap	hoop

In your mind, do you see a picture of **sauce** poured over Killer Krumpets, hear the mixture bubbling in the pot, touch its consistency, smell the chocolate, and taste the sugar? In this instance, sight, smell, and taste are probably the main senses because of their strong associations with food.

What about a **seat** and a **seam**? Which senses do these words stimulate? Sight and touch?

And the **sun**? Sight, and the memory of a painful redness (touch) from that beautiful summer day?

A **sore** looks grim and is unpleasant to touch.

A **seal** might arouse the visual, auditory, and tactile senses while offending the olfactory. It would be unlikely to stimulate the gustatory.

Which sense do you favor? How do you introduce the raw data "out there" to your interpreting system "in here"? By using the mind's eye, via the mind's ear, through touch, or do you use smell or taste? Most often, you use a combination.

GUT 3: Effective memory is a vast *organized* network:

The most effective way to *link* ideas is to *picture* them.

You'll rely on supersonic travel: SST—a combination of
sight, sound, smell plus taste and touch.
Which is your most-used sense?
How do you get a grasp on your reality?
**How do you present your world to your
universal, mighty mind?**

15

The Presents of the Past

Repetition is essential to effective remembering. So let's review.

Anything and everything that has happened to you or has had even the flimsiest contact with your mind must be preserved somehow. The information we are talking about in this *little red book* can be brought back to consciousness at will. In the context of *Yumm,* memory means conscious memory; it is tip-of-the-tongue knowing.

Question: What do I mean by *your* memory?

Answer: It's *your* ability to bring back to mind (recall, remember, recollect)—deliberately, effortlessly, and instantly—any information you choose. This information is a counterpart to your heightened consciousness, expanded knowledge, wider understanding, deepened sensitivity, and broader vision. In short, it's a counterpart to your extended mind.

Memory is not a physical thing; there is no "it" to paint, photocopy, or gift-wrap. Your ability to bring something back to mind could not be X rayed, X-rated, or excommunicated. The art of remembering cannot be hauled into a laboratory, dumped on a scale, and weighed and measured. The science of recollection cannot be wheeled into an operating theatre and inspected or dissected. There is no possible procedure, medical or otherwise, for anesthetizing *the* memory so as to amputate *a* memory. Unlike our (physical) bodies, the process of recall cannot be fallen upon, tickled, bitten, or eaten.

A house is a physical thing. It is limited by solid foundations, defining walls, and building materials combined in various ways. It is embedded firmly in the earth—solid and visible, fixed and inflexible. A house is a triumph not only of construction, but also of careful planning (a very high level of thinking), energetically acted upon. Built systematically from the base up, brick by brick, it is not the astonishing end-product of a dash here and a drop there, of serendipity and chance, of "let's try this" and "maybe that'll do." A permanent house cannot be built with smoke, mirrors, and rats on treadmills. It is not a clever illusion.

Memory is not a physical thing. It is explained loosely as a potentially limitless process centered on a solid and fixed nucleus of knowledge. This nub of knowing grows continuously through the ongoing addition of new information. It is rooted firmly in mind—formless and invisible, fluid and flexible. Conscious memory is a triumph not only of ongoing linking, but also of careful planning (a very high level of thinking), deliberately acted upon. Built systematically from the core out, bit by bit, emotion by emotion, it is not the astonishing end-product of a dash here and a drop there, of serendipity and chance, of "let's try this" and "maybe that'll do." An effective memory cannot be built with smoke, mirrors, and rats on treadmills. It is not a clever illusion.

So memory is many things:

a *concept*—an idea, an abstraction in a dimensionless and invisible world that has no form;
a *positive expectation* (B4?!) that seamlessly becomes a self-fulfilling prophecy;
a *consciousness* that *is* everywhere, but *is* nowhere;
a *process*—ongoing, never-ending, ever-growing, for life; and
a *skill* that can be miraculously developed with deliberate learning.

Not so long ago in the West, we were exhorted to listen closely, understand clearly and discuss logically and concisely. Living was supposed to be a precise, ordered, rational affair. Thinking and behavior were meant to be tidy, neat, and predictable. Being artistic or a dreamer was out; conformity was in. To be creative was somehow suspect. The "three Rs"—reading, 'riting and 'rithmetic—were the traditional Cings of the Klassroom.

But now, to complement this conditioning, there is a spouse atop the Royal House: TLC—thinking, learning, and creativity. Thinking that solves problems presides. Learning that is both useful and ongoing rules. Creativity that is practical is enthroned. But a great leader should also exude another form of *tlc*: tender, *l*oving *c*are.

TLC *and* the three Rs are the present-day monarchs of biotech and high tech, the sovereigns of worldwide communication and other electronic wizardry, the kings of pervasive marketing and global markets. TLC *and* the three Rs are the leaders of all purposeful human evolution.

Most of us yearn to be more creative. But many feel that designers, musicians, painters, writers, and other artistic types have some sort of mysterious and exclusive right to creativity. This is a severely limiting and false belief. Novel insight and innovative thinking are essential ingredients for success. We can all develop these dormant capacities, for there is a dozing giant within each one of us.

Creative imagination is the forging of a link between two previously unconnected ideas for a purpose that might not be apparent at the time. The activity of bringing back to mind, of remembering, thrives on original connections. How can you learn to generate these original ideas; innovate with practical new insight; lead with bold, untried concepts; tread unfamiliar paths, push through to unknown territory; be more imaginative; and think with greater creativity?

Please remain seated, tighten your safety belt, rise, and pay—with attention. You are about to receive the ultimate revelation, the secret of the ages, for the royal road to practical imagination is made of quite basic stuff, really: sand, gravel, tar, you know, that sort of thing. The builders trusted themselves; they simply started. They just did it.

This is your Holy Grail:
Believe in yourself
Simply start
Just do it
Now
!

There are endless possibilities, because creative/imaginative thinking can be learned. In order to develop any skill, we need to practice. In the past we had to be creative just to survive. Today, mere survival is no longer an issue. Unfortunately, many of us have slid into a *rut*. We have fallen into mental habits that are difficult to climb out of. We have allowed ourselves to be herded willy-nilly so that we passively satisfy the desires of others and become indistinguishable in a faceless crowd. We no longer think originally.

To enrich our lives, we should think creatively.

All too many of us are trained to conform to family, job, and marketplace self-interest. This discourages us from being ourselves and looking out for our own highest and best interests. All too often we allow somebody else to take control of our destiny. We are persuaded to be a "good" son or a "helpful" sister, a "hard-working" employee, or a "loyal" consumer. Unceasingly, our culture tempts us onto the commercial treadmill and tempts us to acquire more, and more, specious virtues, superficial qualities, glittery things, pretty crap. Time and again we forget that acquiring and owning also mean upgrading, renewing, replacing…comparing, contrasting, competing…and paying (not with doddle nuts or attention this time, but with hard, after-tax cash).

In truth, we should stop mimicking the clone next to us. He is the one who thinks he is doing the right thing, according to what he has read (usually in the paper) or heard (normally from a friend). He belongs in the past, for he is trapped in obsolete mental patterns. He is in a *rut*.

There are two things that you *will not* be doing: striving for perfection and …nothing. There are two things you *will* be doing: breaking through old limitations and reassessing false beliefs. This will lead you to exciting, uncommon forms of thinking. And you will be generating new ideas and evolving fresh attitudes. Original thoughts are the basis of all progress, growth, and change in everything—from aardvark to zymurgy.

This new thinking will be for a purpose. Creativity—or generating new ideas—enables you to see that old problem in a new light. It is the spark of originality, inspiration, and illumination that successfully blends brazen colors, invents the latest product, arrives at groundbreaking solutions, builds families, forms teams, shows a way ahead, and guides you forward into a better tomorrow.

But creativity also appreciates simplicity, sees things as they really are, feels balanced, is emotionally right, and relieves stress. Most important, this relaxed, lighthearted, spontaneous approach builds a strong, confident, and effective memory.

In addition to your present ways of thinking, I urge you also to start thinking in a different fashion. Many of your ideas should be zany, over-the-top, irreverent, far-out, wacky, crude, and even downright dumb. Increasingly, your thoughts and ideas will become uniquely yours. More of your thinking will be playful, childlike, and fun. As your mental processes become more independent, so will your behavior.

GUT 4: Make your *picturing* and *link structures* uniquely *yours*.

In one sense, memories are *not* gifts; they are rewards.
They are due payment for purposeful and successful effort—
fair exchange for intention supported by consistent and persistent attention.
In another sense, memories *are* gifts:
the presents of the past.

16

The Presence of the Present

All of us have the ability to create mental pictures. A great white shark or a perfect red rose; a pylon, a table, or an elephant—all these words bring images to mind. These are things we remember as visual representations.

That is how we were probably first exposed to them—as pictures in books, at the movies, on TV, in real life. Such information is stored via a mental ability we have chosen to call imagination—our faculty for seeing images. With imagination we photocopy in color, duplicating as close to the original as possible. Although imagination is primarily about the mind's eye, it also includes the other senses. But nothing new is involved. The purpose is merely to reconstruct what was out there, with nothing added and a minimum taken away.

No doubt you can see your home in your mind's eye; you are able to walk through it, room by room. You can visualize your car. Driving (mentally) down to the local shops is easy and natural. In your mind, you can wander down the aisles in your local grocery store, mentally choosing a doughnut here and a jar of doddle nut oil there.

Come to think of it, that supermarket is a very ordered affair, isn't it? But imagine if everything was just thrown helter-skelter onto the floor. The merchandise would be the same, but there would be a total lack of any method or system. Only the visible goods could be found and used. Hardly anything would be accessible. Imagine if all the books in the library...? Pretend that all the things in your kitchen...?

Naah, it doesn't bear thinking about...

A pylon, a table, and an elephant; a doughnut and doddle nut oil? Maybe you do not find these interesting, and therefore not memorable. Our minds demand stimulation and excitement. We need a tiny spark to transform those dull little impressions into something powerful. That small flash will make all the difference.

So let's play it again, Sam. But this time...*with feeling*! To be really memorable, we should drench and enrich information *with emotion*.

Nearly everyone who was over the age of ten when JFK was shot, or when Challenger exploded, or on that ghastly day known as 9/11 remembers precisely where they were when they first heard or saw the news. Each of us was bathed in intense emotion, and emotion makes things memorable. As to the effectiveness of reason only: Can you imagine choosing your spouse or lover on the strength of logic alone?

But first we must give our impressions clear definition. We constantly monitor the world "out there" via data gathered by the senses. These pulses are registered in the mind—for what they are worth. Often we don't make them worth much. Many of our impressions are so faint and foggy that they get lost in the mazes of our mind, just as one person gets swept along in a mob. He is undeniably there, but he cannot be identified as an individual. He is, literally, just part of the mass. If these minute bits of data are allowed to stay fuzzy and ill-defined—nebulous, like hot air—they will always elude us. They will remain without value.

Once they are defined, we must make these impressions distinct from their neighbors; it is not enough that they are precise. When a black-coated man goes out into a crowd of thousands of other black-coated individuals he quickly gets swallowed up. He isn't lost to himself, but we can't find him. Put him in a red jacket and then let him mingle with the black coats and he'll stick out like a bright light in the night.

Similarly, information needs to be both unmistakable and easily recognizable; it must stand out from the throng. The impression needs distinctive clothing; it must be conspicuous. That mental blob must be made memorable. *The most vivid and effective red coat is a strong feeling, an intense emotion.*

To achieve this, we must pay attention, and this payment is a deliberate process. Bringing one's whole mind to bear on something automatically creates interest. Focusing our thoughts is critical to successful remembering. Interest flows from a concentrated mind as surely as the exuberance of spring follows the chilly stasis of deep winter. And the more senses we can involve in the process, the greater the consciousness, the more distinct the impression, and the stronger the interest. This intensity of thought attracts feelings and emotions. Each supports and encourages the other, and so the process continues. Mere impressions become unforgettable.

So now we are faced with a threefold challenge:

First, to stimulate and revitalize our underutilized powers of creative imagination.

Second, to develop and to blend as many senses as possible.

Third, to make the whole message clear and conspicuous by making it sense-rich, feeling-intense, and drenched in emotion. In the realm of the blind, the one-eyed man is king; he has an outstanding attribute that others lack. A redcoat is needed.

We need a skeleton to support these essential aspects of memory. There is such a framework, and you have already started to use it.

May I give you another ten words to remember in sequence?

toes
toad
tin
dam
tire
tail
dish
tick
dove
tap

To help you memorize these items, try this:

Start with **toes**. See them thar toes; hear them crunching on sand, squishing in mud, squashing snails, squelching through warm, melted chocolate; touch stones with them, walk over soft carpeting, or caress silk; smell those benighted digits; and even taste the critters. Experience them. Feel pain, pleasure, amusement, disgust. Get involved with the little brutes. Lose yourself in them. Make them memory-rich. Those mighty mites must develop their own unique personality. They must become an actual breathing presence.

Do the same with a **toad**. See and hear and touch and smell and taste and experience and feel that amphibian. Get involved with and lose yourself in that tailless creature. Make it memory-rich. Fill it with its own, unique personality until it becomes an actual living presence. The beast gains a clear, vivid, real existence in your mind. That enormous frog is now a complete, living picture.

And then a vital step: Link the two pictures in your mind's eye. Make their interaction funny, humorous, crude, vulgar, way-out, over-the-top, profane, wacky, zany. Introduce movement. Exaggerate size. Experience the two presences as being interlinked. Associate your images of the **toes** and the **toad**. If only for a split second, actually see the two images connected—*picture and link* them. Treat them as *your pals.*

But, you say, this is too much like hard work! Continue the process…

Begin with the end in mind. With unfolding understanding—U2—and *me,* visual memory will become vastly more than just a mirror to reflect the past. You will strengthen and enlarge your ability to imagine. You will develop your capacity not only to reconstruct, but also to generate new and often fanciful impressions. You are starting to build a truly unlimited, magnificent memory in order to function more effectively in your everyday life. This could be the start of living a future that you actively create, rather than reliving a past that you passively allowed to be created for you.

Imagine how much better you will feel as you expand your memory. Your confidence will grow. You will become more attractive as an individual. Wallow in that luxurious feeling: "I know that I know." Soak yourself in the relaxed confidence that will come from trusting in your effortless ability to bring back to mind whatever you choose: "I feel better. I love it." Saturate yourself in your quiet inner calm: "I can remember whatever I intend, whenever I choose, wherever I am, whoever I'm with."

Yes, *me* is involved. Remember the Golden Rule: Take it nice 'n' easy. Stay calm and relaxed; effective memory-building is a lifelong process. What is important is that you have committed yourself to a direction. You have made plain your intention—to improve your memory. And you are striving to attain that deep, tranquil state of knowing that you and your inner resources can rise to any occasion. As surely as good memory automatically supports better memory, the respect and recognition of others must follow.

Learning to crawl weren't no cakewalk neither, but the effort was worth it! Do you remember learning to write or to drive, to play tennis or to say Dennis? Can you recall learning to do anything worthwhile? At first, even the essentials were difficult, but with practice it got easier. With time and repetition, you learned more of the skill. It became progressively more automatic. What had been difficult yesterday, was done without thinking today.

One day you realized that the basic process was automatic. A new habit of thought, which was a fresh attitude, had been created. So then you concentrated your mental energy on getting better—on improving—and you focused on being conscious of your life as you experienced it at each moment.

Time waits for nobody; your present moment instantly becomes your past. Now is immediately then. But now is reality. You can function only in this minute slice of time called *now*. When you do, you become enormously inventive, for the simple reason that you have withdrawn yourself from past and future.

All your energy is focused in the present moment. A tremendous explosion must occur, and that eruption is creativity. And that is memorable.

You will be increasingly conscious of the presence of the present.

"Thank you, memory. I know we are a winning team
—everywhere and anywhere, every time, any place…with anyone."

17

The Presence of the Past

Six

<u>G</u>reat <u>U</u>niversal <u>T</u>ruths

Govern the Effective Recall of Information.

Gut 1 Is about Structure.

Throughout the universe there is order. Throughout our mental universe there must also be planning, system, organization, and method.

Gut 2 Is about Links.

The Oh-Zone—Oh, that reminds me—is associating one idea with the next. This gives continuity and form to a bit here and a piece there.

Gut 3 Is about Making (Mental) Pictures.

We are creatures of the "I" and the eye, whether we see the actual, the imagined, or the envisaged.

These three **GUTs** are your p̲icturing a̲nd l̲ink s̲tructures:
your *pals.*

Gut 4 Is about You and Yours.

The way you picture and how you link and organize will be exclusive to you. Such magical processes can only have an ownership of one; they are original and unique…to you. No one else can know your thinking or think your thinking.

Your *pals* are *yours,* and *yours* alone.

Always remember *your pals.*

Gut 5 Is about Fun.

Have a good time; enjoy yourself. Your pals should evoke memories of fun and laughter, camaraderie and companionship. That's why they're your buddies.

Have *fun* with *your pals.*

GUT 6 Is about Trust.

As your belief in the capacity of your mind magnifies, as your confidence in your ability to remember grows, as the vigor of your whole thinking process intensifies, as your expectation of a more effective memory increases, so you will automatically come to rely on your mind and its infinite capacity to recall. You will learn to trust yourself, and life itself.

Trust in and have fun with your pals.

Six
Great Universal Truths
govern the effective recall of information:
trust in and have fun with your pals.

Six
Great Universal Truths
ensure that your chosen memories will be an unforgettable presence:
the presence of the past.

PART THREE
A WORM'S-EYE VIEW—
SPECIFIC TOOLS AND
TECHNIQUES

18

Your Days Are Numbered

Today's world is addicted to acquiring more technology, more technical toys, and more tools. Always we want more, and always we want more things. In some ways this is good; our lives are being made easier and better. But these everyday servants have a nasty habit of creeping up and somehow becoming our masters. They come at a price, over and above just hard, after-tax money.

As life becomes increasingly complex, our identity is being lost in quantity: mass production, mass packaging, mass distribution, mass merchandising, mass markets. You and I are being lost in the crowd, in the sheer volume of mass. We become statistics, electronic bits, data entries, incomprehensible codes. In a world that is becoming less personal, we are no longer individuals. We are merely units in a specialist niche, aspects of a market, a typical (or rogue) profile, elements within a target segment, mindless shoppers, faceless consumers.

To our bank we are an account number. Before a machine will give us our own money, we must enter "our" personal identity number. Our homes are numbers with a home-loan company or a landlord. We have an address that is number-based. Our telephone has probably a seven-digit number, with more numbers for area, region, and country. Our transport system is identified by an alphanumeric license number and really owned by a finance company through contract numbers. We have the possession and use of some of our furniture and fittings, subject to full and final payment involving deferred-sale organizations and their agreement numbers.

We are only a tiny blip of digitalized data.

All too often, you and I are locator ciphers and access codes. We buy stock codes and reference numbers through individual identity modules and account numbers. As a Cash Sale, Credit Card Transaction, or Account Code, we are automatically and electronically recognized by Serial Number, awarded a Bonus, sent to Inventory Deduction, included in a Sales Report, absorbed into Market Analysis, assigned a Promotional Category, given a Segment Profile, added to QuikRetrieval, sold to Encryption, and urged to "Have a nice day."

Our very identity is just a number.

Events happen on the 19th of the 4th; these goods should be consumed before 11/25 (though today is 09/15); be at 34, 23rd Street at 15H00; read it on page 298; buy item 934/38 for 498,39 with a 0,5% discount if paid within 14 days. You might be 223 and 5' 10" and have a minus of 4298,46 that has already been spent, with 5701.54 still available. Your health scheme will not acknowledge your very existence until you confess to being 9464829-5372-00. To local government, you have no rights until you own up to being 893401/56.81. The revenue authorities are not interested in the tiresome detail of your name … 'What is your tax number?'

Your days are numbered.

Our world is increasingly number-based. We are explained, interpreted, measured, judged, encouraged, and hounded…in terms of numbers. More and more, numbers define our lives. More and more, numbers describe our very existence.

We are not passive brutes. We have developed all sorts of mechanisms to remind us of these numbers. Personal computers and PDAs, time management systems and diaries, and bits of boxes are all useful aids. But sometimes they are not available or appropriate. Maybe your colleague is not around when you need a particular e-mail address. It is possible that your spouse has also forgotten that reference number that you need right now. What happens if your lover never knew your flight number in the first place? But this is not the real issue.

Surely you owe it to yourself to be as independent as possible, to strive to gain control over the normal, ordinary detail of your life. Do you really enjoy scratching frenetically in your handbag for "that little bit of paper" or searching for an elusive assistant? Spending minimal time and a little effort in learning how to remember numbers is an invaluable investment in the source of it all:

you. Surely you owe it not only to them out there," but also—and more impor-
tantly—to you "in here" to know, and to know that you know. It feels so good.

Numbers are soulless little squiggles that have no emotional appeal. They are
funny designs that mean nothing to our minds. Aunt Mabel's telephone number neither ignites my imagination nor inflames my passions. Few of us can
relate to mere digits. They are impersonal and do not elicit any form of human
response. Numerals are part of a world in which few of us feel at home. But
they are crucial. Like it or not, numbers are of increasing importance to each
one of us.

However, a number has one huge, universal advantage: It is absolute. Words
have shades of meaning that cannot be nailed down. Numbers are exact. In
combination with other numbers, they can be used to perform precise calcula-
tions and give unvarying results. And their range is infinite. Numbers are ideal
for pinpoint accuracy, everywhere and every time. And they are an essential
and ever-growing focus of our lives. We need to remember more and more
numbers of numbers…

About 350 years ago, a system was devised to help us remember numbers. This
method has been changed and improved many times over the intervening
years, and known by many names.

I call this structure the *Sound* System.

19

Groping about in the
Wonderful World of Why

A gospel is a body of teaching considered to be of great importance.

Let me introduce myself. My name is Robin, and I am the author of this *little red book*. The next couple of pages are fundamental to the whole gospel of mind and memory. I would like this to be a personal chat, just you and me— mind to mind—so to speak.

The past decade and a half has been an incredible adventure for me. At about the age of forty, I realized that I needed a complete career change. Wherever the future took me, I would need a very high degree of personal fulfillment in my new occupation. I knew that I would have to be flexible to deal with the inevitable challenges that occur at an ever-increasing rate in a fast-changing world. I also knew that I would have to rely largely on my own resources. An accelerated process of ongoing self-education would further develop my knowledge and skills; my self-confidence needed the boost. But there is no reliable map for unexplored territory.

Success has two sides: material possessions and personal fulfillment. Symbols of prestige no longer motivated me that strongly. I knew that as long as I offered value and service, and kept a wary eye on my spending habits, money had to follow. And money *is* vitally important. But I came to understand that I needed the flip side as well: a life filled with meaning—the ongoing, creative accomplishment of aims that were both my own, and worthy.

My personal odyssey really began when I started to look within. I simply asked myself a couple of questions: What really excites me, and what do I find truly satisfying? This journey, begun years ago, continues to be remarkable. A single sentence can sum up my progress over the last fifteen years: I am thinking, at last.

For the first time in my life, I have been using my mind to plan ahead and be proactive. I have worked out what is truly important to me. I am creating my own future, because I now know that my destiny is in my hands. Weak, I am of little value to myself and unlikely to be of ongoing and meaningful service to anyone else. As a strong, secure person, I can be of benefit to others. When all is said and done, that is the source of true satisfaction.

For me, doubts seemed to walk hand-in-hand with learning. After all, I was leaving behind the early, energy-driven times of my life for a later phase where experience and good judgment should play a greater role. Yet I did not feel that I was retaining information as effectively as I should. The sense of a basic cohesion and structure to my expanding fund of knowledge was missing. I did not think I was becoming a little smarter. I reckoned that my ability to recall should be more efficient than when I was younger. Could it be that my mind was more of a patched parachute than a nifty network? And so I groped about in the wonderful World of Why.

The more I questioned, the more powerfully I was led down the path of memory. As I explored this trail, I began to appreciate the power of emotion and the value of structured imagination. Herd these three, shepherd the whole process purposefully—what is called "thinking"—and the effects can be awesome. Mind is a vast, integrated presence. All the different facets are crucial to the effective working of the whole. The result is far mightier than the sum of the individual parts.

A mind embedded in disciplined emotion, unlimited thanks to creative imagination and guided by wise thinking, is impressive. Such a mind notices and remembers a great deal. The *Sound* System steers you to this type of mind, for it is a planned framework that evolves over time. It demands new imaginings and supporting emotion. With practice, the *Sound* System is an edifice that works with progressively more of the mind. In time, with repetition, the whole of mind becomes intricately involved.

This system should be much more than merely a method for remembering numbers. At first, it can be used to recall numerals. With time and practice, the net is cast far wider. The *Sound* System evolves into a whole-brain development program:

The *me* of *m*ental *e*xercise is a worm's-eye view. This precedes memory expansion.

The *me* of *m*emory *e*xpansion is a bird's-eye view. This complements mind extension.

The *me* of *m*ind *e*xtension is a global view. This can whirl out infinitely to...a universal view?

A cosmonaut in orbit can see our whole planet, as well as a vast, ordered galaxy beyond. Such an endless, splendid panorama raises big issues and stimulates big thinking. Could that be...astrothaut?

All that we can ever comprehend of the universe must reside within our own minds. Your conception of your universe must dwell within your mind. Whatever you do with your life is your decision. Whether you make or break your world is your choice. You can choose to make the *Sound* System your own Space Shuttle program—the tool for realizing your big thinking, your magnificent voyage.

You are the cosmonaut of your own reality.
The *Sound* System is the ideal craft.
Why not launch yourself?
Could this be the start of, umm...
astrothaut?

20

The *Sound* System

What is the primary aim of the Sound System?

By converting numerals into pictures,

the Sound *System enables you*

to remember numbers.

This is the most advanced and the most versatile of all the methods of improving memory, embracing four major benefits:

- A precise plan of action for recalling numbers to a limitless extent is the first benefit.

- A systematic technique for recollecting long lists: people, things, events, "to-do" is the second benefit.

- A template for remembering where things are is the third benefit. For example, what the 34th item on the list is and what number Jane is on the list; what is on page 22 and where that photograph is on a page; the layout of the middle page, and so on.

- A crucible for stimulating your creative imagination is the fourth benefit. This is conclusive. By its very nature, the *Sound* System will force you to function unconventionally in the mental sense. It also demands that your whole mind/brain be involved, so your entire psyche will be fully engaged.

Every number from 0 to 36,895,654.74 and beyond is a combination of only ten numerals, 0 to 9. The English language is made up of the 26 letters of the alphabet—the building blocks of words. These building blocks are divided into 21 consonants and 5 vowels.

The consonants can be grouped into ten basic sounds. In the *Sound* System, each of the ten digits is assigned one of the ten basic consonant sounds.

These consonant sounds are then combined with *vowels* and the letters *w, h,* and *y (why)* to convert numbers into simple things—everyday stuff that we can easily picture in mind. So meaningless, unmemorable scribbles—numbers—are converted into a form that can be seen in the mind's eye and heard in the mind's ear. Deliberately mixed with feeling, these things-as-numbers are now meaningful and memorable. In fact, they become unforgettable.

This, and what follows, is confusing at first. Just browse through it now...and again. It'll soon make sense. I've already mentioned that the *Sound* System is the broadest and most sophisticated aid to memory. Take a few minutes to grasp the basics of this system; they really are very, very simple. For its part, the *Sound* System will reward your efforts lavishly.

Make it *your intention to pay attention, consistently and persistently.* Use the golden rules of staying calm, confident, and relaxed, and use repetition, repetition, repetition...practice, with *me.* By *trusting in and having fun with your pals,* you will be able to recall numbers effortlessly—and endlessly!

The *Sound* System is also awkward to explain on paper. As an example, imagine writing to a friend and trying to describe, in detail, how to stir a cup of tea using a tool called a teaspoon. To show someone face to face would take a few seconds. It would be the easiest thing in the world. But to explain in writing is very cumbersome.

Now, back to work. Let's look at these ten consonant sounds. How can they be classified into only **ten groups?**

Group 0:
Take the letters soft c as in cell, s as in sew, and z as in zero—c, s, and z. Actually say the words out loud. Notice how the first consonant of each is formed by the controlled exhalation of air—c and s hiss when air is expelled, whereas z resonates or vibrates over the tongue. These three consonants make up only two sounds (c and s are the same, as in cease and sauce).

    soft c
    s_
    z

Group 1:
How about d, t, and th—dot, tot, and thong? Again, say them out loud. All three are similar sounds, made with a sort of click from the roof of your mouth.

    d
    t_
    th

The next four "groups" are very simple because they contain only one sound each.

Group 2:
    n
    (nun)

Group 3:
    m
    (mum)

Group 4:
    r
    (rut)

Group 5:
    l
    (lad)

Group 6:
This is the biggest family of sounds and causes the most difficulty.

Say soft g (as in gem); dge (as in hedge); j (as in jaw); ch (chop); tch (hatch); and sh (show). Because soft g, dge, and j (gem, hedge, and jaw) are the same, as are ch and tch (chop and hatch), with the sh (show) separate, there are only three different sounds within this group.

> soft g
> dge
> j_
> ch
> tch_
> sh

Group 7:

Now pronounce hard c (cow), k (key), hard g (go), and qu (queue). Here, too, there are only three sounds (cow and key are the same) so we have c/k, g, and qu.

> hard c
> k_
> hard g_
>
> qu

Group 8:

Now try f (as in foe), ph (phone), and v (as in vow). Two of these sounds are made by breathing out through pursed lips—f and ph are the same.

> f
> ph_
> v

Group 9:

The final group of sounds is b (bay) and p (pay)—a mild explosion of air is puffed out through opened lips.

> b
> p

All the consonant sounds in the English language are included in these ten groups, except for *w, h,* and *y* (*why*). The letter h only has some value if it changes the sound of other consonants, as in th, ch, ph, and sh.

For the moment, just try to remember this summary of what you have read so far:

c and s; z	0
d and t; th	1
n	2
m	3
r	4
l	5
soft g, dge and j; ch and tch; sh	6
hard c and k; hard g; qu	7
f and ph; v	8
b; p	9

Now think back to those lists that you memorized. Recall the second list of ten items:

hose
hat
hen
home
hair
hill
hedge
hook
hive
hoop

Remember, the letters *w*, *h*, and *y* (*why*) and the *vowels* are used to make the consonant sounds into words. So, in the word "hose," neither the "h-" (*why*) nor the "-o-" (a *vowel*) have any value—they are there just to give the "-se" meaning. And the "se" is a zzzz-sound, which equals or represents the number 0.

This list represents these numbers:

hose	0
hat	1
hen	2
home	3
hair	4
hill	5
hedge	6
hook	7
hive	8
hoop	9

Similarly,

sauce	00
seat	01
sun	02
seam	03
sore	04
seal	05
sash	06
sock	07
safe	08
soap	09

And,

toes	10
toad	11
tin	12
dam	13
tire	14
tail	15
dish	16
tick	17
dove	18
tap	19

Now test yourself. What numbers could this list represent?

> nose
> net
> nun
> gnome
> Nero
> nail
> niche
> neck
> knife
> knob

Let's take nose: you know that "n-" equals 2; "-o-" being a *vowel,* is just a filler letter; and "-se" (the sound is zzzz) represents 0. So the word, and the mental picture of a **nose**, is the number 20.

Net is 21, and so on.

Always remember that this is the *Sound* System: What is important is how a consonant *sounds,* not how it looks.

The g of gnome is silent; the word is pronounced nome.

Similarly, there is a silent k in the words pronounced nife and nob.

Although Nero is both two syllables (near and Oh) and a name, I feel that it meets the criteria of "easy-to-picture and quite distinct."

How can you remember which *sound* represents which number?

Here is a very easy aid to memory:

digit	consonant (sound)	memory aid (or mnemonic)
0	soft c and s; z	imagine three snakes, curled in the shapes of a c, an s, and a z, in a big, round frying pan
1	d; t; th	d and t have one down-stroke; the first letter of th also has one down-stroke
2	n	two down-strokes
3	m	three down-strokes
4	r	there are four letters in "four"— and the last letter is rrrrr
5	l	L forms the top of 5
6	soft g, dge, and j; ch and tch; sh	reverse a j and it looks like a 6 (it's a long shot, but this is the tricky family of sounds)
7	hard c and k; g; qu	the letter k is made up of two 7s
8	f and ph; v	a flowing, handwritten f with two hoops looks like an 8 (what about the Ford V8 motor?), and
9	b; p	p is an upside-down b and a mirror-image 9.

Here are some mnemonics or memory aids that can help you to remember all of the sounds that go together in each sound grouping:

digit	mnemonic
0	Nothing ceases
1	One at death
2	n-sound only
3	m-sound only
4	r-sound only
5	l-sound only
6	Six charge show judge hatch
7	Seven go cook quick
8	Eight vie for phone
9	Nine babies pop

By now, you may be a little overwhelmed. Please don't worry. You are just beginning to grasp what the *Sound* System is all about.

Take it nice 'n' easy.

Do a little learning and put in some practice every day.

You will understand this method sooner than you think, and you will master it more easily than you can imagine.

21

More Sounds from the System

The purpose of the Sound *System*

is to help us

remember numbers

by *converting numerals into pictures;*

by converting *numerals into pictures;*

by converting numerals *into pictures;*

by converting numerals into *pictures;*

by converting numerals into pictures.

The production of any speech sound (or any sound at all) involves the movement of a stream of air. Every language of the world contains the two basic classes of speech sounds, called consonants and vowels. In producing consonants, the current of air is restricted at some point as it flows through the mouth. A vowel, on the other hand, has no significant obstruction. Bearing this in mind, let me repeat the basics of the *Sound* System.

The *Sound* System is phonetic: Each number from 0 to 9 is represented by a consonant sound. The letters *w, h,* and *y* (*why*) and the *vowels* are used as fillers to make the consonant sounds into a word.

It is essential to grasp that this system is *phonetic.* It is based on what is *heard* and not on the way the word looks. Spelling is irrelevant. The letters themselves are not important. The *Sound* System is *ear-based*—it relies on *the sense of hearing. Hear here.*

Numbers are without meaning. They do not convey ideas or create pictures for the mind to interpret. They don't appeal to any of our senses, so they have no sensory quality. There is no emotional interest; the imagination is not stimulated in any way. Numerals almost seem to be designed to be forgotten. In order to make them memorable, you must give them meaning. You do this by encoding numbers into words. These words are easily borne in mind in picture form. And then you *trust in and have fun with our pals.* How do you do this?

There are ten basic consonant sounds in English. Our Arabic counting system has ten different numerals. Each consonant sound is matched with a number from zero to nine. Using *why* and the *vowels*, these consonants are fleshed out into words. These words should be of simple objects that can be imagined effortlessly and instantly. They must be unmistakable, every time. Recall the item and you remember the number. With a little practice, these (mental) pictures automatically represent the numbers we choose to remember.

Here is a list of every number from 00 to 99:

00 sauce	0 hose	10 toes	20 nose	30 mouse	40 rose
01 seat	1 hat	11 toad	21 net	31 mat	41 road
02 sun	2 hen	12 tin	22 nun	32 moon	42 rain
03 seam	3 home	13 dam	23 gnome	33 mom	43 ram
04 sore	4 hair	14 tire	24 Nero	34 mare	44 rear
05 seal	5 hill	15 tail	25 nail	35 mole	45 roll
06 sash	6 hedge	16 dish	26 niche	36 match	46 roach
07 sock	7 hook	17 tick	27 neck	37 mug	47 rake
08 safe	8 hive	18 dove	28 knife	38 movie	48 roof
09 soap	9 hoop	19 tap	29 knob	39 mop	49 rope
50 lace	60 jazz	70 case	80 face	90 bus	
51 light	61 jet	71 coat	81 foot	91 boat	
52 line	62 john	72 cane	82 phone	92 bone	
53 lamb	63 jam	73 comb	83 foam	93 beam	
54 lyre	64 jar	74 car	84 fire	94 bear	
55 lily	65 jail	75 coal	85 fowl	95 bell	
56 lash	66 judge	76 cage	86 fish	96 badge	
57 leg	67 jug	77 cake	87 fake	97 bike	
58 leaf	68 jive	78 cuff	88 fife	98 beef	
59 lip	69 jab	79 cap	89 fob	99 babe	

I have evolved the list over many years. I find each item clear and simple to pic-ture. With experience, you may gradually modify your mental images to what suits you best. Until you are very familiar with the *Sound* System, I strongly recommend that you stick to these objects. However, this series is far from fixed. For example, 27 does not have to be ne<u>ck</u>. It could be any of the follow-ing: ha<u>nk</u>y, ho<u>nk</u>, I<u>n</u>ca, i<u>nk</u>, <u>n</u>ag, <u>n</u>i<u>ck</u>, <u>n</u>ook, or wi<u>nk</u>. The number 50 might be ha<u>ll</u>s, hai<u>ls</u>, hi<u>ll</u>s, <u>l</u>ace, <u>l</u>a<u>ss</u>, <u>l</u>ease, <u>l</u>ice, <u>l</u>ou<u>se</u>, wa<u>ll</u>s, or ye<u>ll</u>s. Just be aware that every numeral has a whole range of choices.

Make sure that each image is represented by an object that is simple and clearly recognizable. My picture of a <u>s</u>u<u>n</u> (02) is a full circle, while <u>moon</u> (32) is a crescent. <u>Mouse</u> is my word for 30. To avoid any possible confusion with another rodent, 41 is not <u>r</u>a<u>t</u>, but <u>r</u>oa<u>d</u>. My 41 (a <u>r</u>oa<u>d</u>) is very different from my 52 (a <u>l</u>i<u>n</u>e). For num-bers in the sixties I wanted to stay within the "j" group. For 60 I use <u>j</u>a<u>zz</u> and simply see a trumpet, 62 is <u>j</u>oh<u>n</u>—a toilet, <u>j</u>i<u>ve</u> is 68 and a dancer, while 69 is a <u>j</u>a<u>b</u>—a syringe or injection. <u>Fake</u> is 87, where I picture a painting, and a <u>fob</u> (89) is the chain that attaches a watch to a waistcoat. To me, <u>beef</u> (98) is simply a cow.

Since this is the *Sound* System, the emphasis on *sounds* is essential. So, different letters or letter combinations can produce the same sounds:

the letters **ce** (o<u>ce</u>an), **ci** (gra<u>ci</u>ous), **t** (ra<u>t</u>io), **ti** (na<u>ti</u>on) and **s** (<u>s</u>ugar) all make the same **sh** sound, and each of b<u>oar</u>, b<u>ore</u>, d<u>oor</u>, f<u>our</u> and m<u>aw</u> have the same **or** sound.

But the same letter or letter combinations can also take on different sounds:

the **c** in a<u>c</u>t and a<u>ce</u>; the **ch** in <u>ch</u>ur<u>ch</u> versus <u>ch</u>ronic; the **g** in a<u>g</u>o and a<u>ge</u>, or <u>g</u>a<u>ge</u>; the **gh** in <u>gh</u>ost rather than rou<u>gh</u>; the **ng** in si<u>ng</u> as opposed to si<u>ng</u>e; the **s** in <u>s</u>on and <u>s</u>ure; and the **t** in ra<u>t</u>io, as against pa<u>t</u>io.

Combinations of letters can sound like capital letters:

the letters **au** can be capital A as in g<u>au</u>ge; capital O as in g<u>au</u>che; **ow** as in g<u>au</u>cho or **or** as in g<u>au</u>ze.

And you thought Shanghai Chinese might be tricky!

Some *sounds* are tricky to classify and so encode into a number:

The letter x has two consonant sounds, k and s, as in a<u>x</u>e, which is 70. But x can also be a z—<u>x</u>y<u>l</u>o<u>ph</u>o<u>n</u>e—which is 0582.

The **ng** of sing is usually treated as two different sounds—an <u>n</u> and a **g** (27). <u>Sing</u> is 027. <u>Singe</u>, however, equals 026. The two important considerations are that you go by what you *hear* and that you be *consistent*.

Remember that it is the sound that is all-important,

so a<u>ngl</u>e is 275, a<u>ng</u>e<u>l</u> is 265, and e<u>ngage</u> is 276.

When a repeated consonant makes only one sound, it counts as a single digit:

a<u>mass</u> is 30, not 300; <u>tatt</u>y is 11 and not 111, whereas <u>zillion</u> is 052, not 0552, and <u>pall</u> is 95, as are <u>pal</u> and <u>bale</u>.

When a repeated consonant demands two distinct sounds it counts as two digits:

e<u>cc</u>e<u>ntric</u> is 702147!

Two different consonants together make up only one numeral if they create only one sound:

a<u>ck</u>-a<u>ck</u> is 77 and not 7777; a<u>cqu</u>i<u>r</u>e is 74 and not 774; <u>sc</u>e<u>n</u>e, and <u>s</u>ee<u>n</u>, are 02.

A silent consonant is ignored:

<u>limb</u> is 53 and <u>limp</u> is 539, whereas <u>limber</u> is 5394; both <u>could</u> and <u>caught</u> are 71 (and so are <u>ghett</u>o and <u>Keith</u>), whereas <u>cauldron</u> equals 75142 and <u>caulk</u> (and <u>cork</u>) represent 77; <u>sc</u>e<u>n</u>e is 02, not 072, though <u>scan</u> is 072; and <u>flame</u> and <u>phlegm</u> have the same value at 853.

As a final illustration of *the difference between sound and sight,* browse through the following array:

number	sound	example
0	c	cease (00), scent cent sent (021), cession (062), cyst (001)
	s_	say (0), sax (070), scion (02), Scot (071), screw (074), tossed (101)
	z	as (0), scissors (0040), Xerox (0470), zephyr (084)
1	d_	dad, daddy, death (11)
	t	tat, tatty, tooth (11), tatters (1140)
	th	that, tithe (11), thigh (1), thinner (124), thither (114),
2	n	ant (21), gnome (23), knee (2), onion (22), winner (24)
3	m	hammer (34), human (32), Miami (33), resume (403)
4	r	art, ought (41), colonel (7425), error (44), wharf (48), quarry(74)
5	l	elk (57), lacquer (574), lilt (551), loyal (55)
6	soft g	exaggerate (70641), gene (62), ginger (6264), gage (76)
	dge	hodgepodge (696)
	j_	hedge (6), jacks (670), judge (66), vision (862)
	ch	cello (65), conscious (7260), Czech (67), hitch (6)
	tch_	patch (96)
	sh	anxious (2760), cautious(7460), machine (362), show (6), special (0965), sure (64)
7	hard c	account (721), cay, echo (7), icon (72)
	k_	exam (703), chaos (70), quay (7) coke, kayak, khaki (77), knock (27),
	hard g_	gagged, (771)
	qu	choir (74), qualm (743), queue (7)
8	f	five (88), hyphen (82), off (8), rough (48), Stefan (0182)
	ph_	phew (8), phone (82), Daphne (182), Stephen (0182)

	v	of (8), savvy (08), valve (858), Steven (0182)
9	b_	bibbed (991), hob (9)
	p	pipped (991), hop (9).

I suggest that you learn the number-sound equivalents and then just wander through this material a few times. Try to do this a couple of times a day for a week or so. With a little at a time, nice 'n' easy, the principles will become clear and fixed in your mind. Once you understand it, the *Sound* System is straight-forward—a challenge, and fun.

So far you have learned 100 words—all of them *objects*—that cover all numbers from 00 to 99. (You have also learned the ten single digits 1 to 9). When you learn an additional ten items—all of them *colors*—the System expands to embrace a third digit and cover all numbers from 000 to 999.

How?

In order to recall the numeral 84, you would have a picture of a fire in mind. To bring the number 684 to tongue-tip, you would have an image of an orange fire, where the 6 is represented by the color orange. Using the principles of the *Sound* System, the j/ge sound of orange equals 6.

Here is the list of colors:

0	green
1	white
2	blue
3	black
4	red
5	yellow
6	orange
7	silver
8	gold
9	pink

Of course, there is a simple way to remember these colors:

digit	color	memory aid
0	green	imagine the green of an oval sports field
1	white	white has one down-stroke in the *Sound* System
2	blue	two and blue rhyme
3	black	picture the three black prongs of a trident
4	red	the last letter of four is **rrrr**...so **rrrred**
5	yellow	the l-sound of five in the *Sound* System
6	orange	the j-sound of orange in the *Sound* System
7	silver	think of the hissing sounds of **ssseven** and **sssilver**
8	gold	the Golden G-eight in San Francisco
9	pink	the p-sound of the *Sound* System

First you learned 100 words that cover all numbers from 00 to 99. Then you added ten colors to expand the system to three digits—000 to 999.

Now, when you remember another ten words—all *adjectives* (describing words)—the System immediately extends to include a fourth numeral, covering every number from 0000 to 9999.

How?

Let's say that you want to remember the number 6182, which is your four-digit personal identity number. Merely bring a picture of a huge, white phone to mind, for that translates into 6182. Does that make sense? The number 6 has been assigned the sound of **ge**, as in hu**ge**, 1 represents the **t**, as in whi**te**, and phone is the sound-object—the word—we use for 82. To store such a number in memory, merely create a clear, strong mental picture. To remind yourself that a huge, white phone is your PIN, imagine your usual ATM as a phone booth...and you've just answered that phone to be told you've won $1 million. Or whatever works for you.

The list of adjectives follows. *All* obey the sounds of the *Sound* System:

digit	adjective	mnemonic
0	icy	the s-sound of the Sound System
1	wet	one down-stroke
2	new	two down-strokes
3	my	three down-strokes
4	hairy	the r-sound
5	oily	the l-sound
6	huge	the j-sound
7	weak	the k-sound
8	heavy	the v-sound
9	happy	the p-sound

At last you have the capacity to remember any number of up to four digits (0000 to 9999) in one mental bite.

Do you see how these words, as a single picture in mind, represent the numbers?

A hairy, pink neck is…4927;

an oily, blue cap is…5279; and

an icy, gold roof is…0848.

How would you see these numbers:

7118, 2073, and 8514?

What about a weak, white dove;

a new, green comb; and

a heavy, yellow tire?

Which image ties up with which number?

1330…a huge, red nose

3619…a wet, black mouse

6420…my orange tap

Using the lists, what numbers do these pictures represent?

a huge, blue face

my white rose

a happy, black hen

And what colorful and distinct mental impression do these numbers invoke:

4011, 7371, and 6959?

(The answers are on the next page.)

Try to picture a 1066—a wet, green judge; or a 1776—a wet, silver cage; or a 911—a pink toad. Not your usual everyday experience, you will agree. But this is one of the great benefits of the *Sound* System. You will be moving beyond what you experience in the world "out there" and into a universe of your own creation. And the act of creation is essentially the same as that of memorizing—the forging of links between two previously unassociated ideas.

Trust in and have fun with your pals.

6280,

3140, and

932. (Remember, he*n* is 2 because *why* and the vowels are only there so the consonant sounds can be made into a word; 02 would be sau*ce*.)

A hairy, green toad;

a weak, black coat; and

a huge, pink lip.

How do you go about learning the *Sound* System?

You might copy the list of 110 items onto 11 blank cards; one for each grouping: 00–09, 1–9 through 90–99. Each card would have the ten objects next to their numbers (like I've done on page 95). On the back, you'd write the adjective and the color (on the back of 60–69, you'd write huge and orange). You'd carry these prompt cards with you at all times.

With consistent and persistent *me* and *Peat, peat, and more peat,* you'd soon be able to leave them permanently in the drawer at home.

At that stage, you would truly know the *Sound* System.

22

The Presence of
The *Sound* System

How does the *Sound* System work for you and me?

As an extreme example, let's say that you want to remember the 12-digit numeral 490910923875.

You would move through the following steps:

Break the number into bite-sized chunks of four digits each: 4909 1092 3875—or wherever you are most at home, memorywise.

Translate 4909 into *Sound* System-ese: Start by calling to mind your picture of soap (09).

[This image should be vivid and unmistakable. An object is always easier to see than an idea; a cake of soap can be pictured more readily than, say, the act of washing or the concept of hygiene.]

Make this cake of soap a striking pink (909).

Make your striking pink cake of soap conspicuously hairy (4909).

[Hairy, pink soap—that's the order in which we would say it—adjective, color, and object. So let's keep it that way, always!]

Link your impression of hairy, pink soap with a simple and clear image of a wet, green bone (1092).

Finally, link a wet, green bone to my gold coal (3875).

In order to recall the original twelve-digit number, merely bring the single

sequence—the daisy chain—back to mind and convert back to numerals.

[On paper, this is complicated. But let me ask you to do something. Imagine writing to a friend and explaining in detail how he or she should wink, wiggle a toe, or waggle a finger. The written word can be very inefficient. Remember stirring that cup of tea? Ideally, I should give you a few minutes of personal instruction. Failing this, *Yumm* is the best way to learn this invaluable new skill.]

Let me repeat the picturing and linking process (in slightly different words from page 52). In your mind's eye, you create a clear-cut image, and then another. You then associate, in any memorable way, the first vivid picture with the second unmistakable image, the second with the third, the third with the fourth, and so on. That's all…a simple, step-by-step process.

A chain is only as strong as its weakest link. In memory terms, the images *and* their interlinking must be unambiguous. Both the mental pictures themselves and the interaction between them must form a single, unbroken flow—a daisy chain. Then each person in the group, each item on the list, each event in the sequence will be memorable. With practice, it becomes automatic…second nature.

There is another very powerful way to remember things in order: by using the mind's ear. Let's go back to the 12-digit number. Repeat to yourself "hairy, pink soap." Hear yourself say the words. You will be creating an aural, as opposed to a visual, reminder. I have found that logical, rational thinkers tend to favor their mind's ear. Usually this has come at a price: Their creative imagination is underdeveloped. In using the mind's ear (what is called auditory memory) as well as the mind's eye (visual memory), you will be creating another "hook" to help you re-find the original impression.

Remember this? "Both mind and memory can be seen as a three-dimensional net, with the knots representing individual thoughts and ideas, and the strings standing for the associations. No thought is isolated or stands alone. Everything must be joined to something else with knots and ties. These connections are like threads attached to the idea. When you want a particular idea, you must pull the right string. If it has two strings, you double the chance of finding it. If there were twenty strings attached to the thought, you would have a much greater likelihood of finding an effective one to pull."

Your memory, a component of your mind, is also a multisensory process.

You might have difficulty with the colors. In acquiring any new skill, the "secret" is intelligent repetition. A little regularly is the seed of automatic behavior. With practice, the formidable becomes everyday and routine, and a new habit is born.

If you have a "problem" color, look for that elusive hue in your day-to-day dealings and focus on it. We live in a riot of everyday color: cars, signs, billboards, books, magazines, clothes…every shade imaginable. Observe a color you wish to record, then look away and try to reproduce it in your mind's eye. Do this sort of exercise until you are very proficient with that color.

I doubt that you will have any trouble seeing *black* or *white* in your mind's eye. Why? Because they are so common and absolute that you have internalized them unconsciously. *Silver* might mean strength without blemish: stainless steel. Few folk have a problem imagining *gold*. Could it be because we are conditioned to see the metal as highly desirable?

Color can often be felt as a mood, a state of mind. *Blue* Mondays and "the blues" have little to do with shade or hue. *Red* could be the emotion of excitement and passion. You may choose to evoke *pink* more as a feeling—of femininity of giving, loving, and sharing—than of a color.

What about *green, yellow, orange*? Call to mind the different colors; see them, play with them.

The foregoing ideas are mine. You are different. All I am trying to do is to point you in another direction, to suggest some new possibilities, and to put a stamp of approval on mental processes that the ever-present "they" have routinely scorned as being airy-fairy and irrational. As you have with *your pals,* make the *Sound* System *yours.*

The adjectives are also fun. Let's start with *icy.* At first, you will probably be a little stilted and imagine the object as being frozen solid or set in a block of ice. With practice, you might picture something covered in white frost, which is not as fixed and rigid. In time, try to make *icy* a feeling. Actually take ice out of an ice bucket and hold it in your closed fist. Rub it on your forearms. Stroke it around your face. Suck an ice cube. Do this a few times. Really get used to the sensation of being frozen so that you can feel it, at will, to the very core of your being. Let the awareness of ice—the consciousness of freezing and of the state of being frozen—become a very real, readily identifiable sensation. With time and repetition, at the deliberate flick of a mental switch, you will be able to actually turn on or experience the feeling of iciness. You'll have expanded your mind. No sweat.

Do the same with *wet*. Initially you may only be able to see an item half-submerged, representing wetness. Your picture will probably be concrete and inflexible. With time and practice your imagination will become more fluid. Wet might be droplets, as seen on the side of a frosted glass. Wet might even become a feeling. Your whole thinking process will be more free-wheeling, fun, and inventive. There is no right or wrong—only calm, confident, relaxed fun…and efficient remembering.

For *new*, what about in mint condition, pristine or unused, or maybe just restored? With time and practice, new might become a perception of freshness, the quality of being untouched, exciting, or original. Explore your imagination; be adventurous and innovative. Search. Dig. Find new meanings; look for different interpretations. Be curious; be creative.

My is a magic mind-expander. At first you might need to see a hand in place. That would represent your hand and my. But *my* can be intensely emotional; it is the joy of possession and the pride of ownership: "This is mine." With focused repetition, my soon becomes a real presence, a strong feeling: "This is a part of me." And that is memorable. Feel the pleasure of ownership in my green bus (3090).

And for the next two: *hairy* and *oily* can be seen, or felt, or tasted, or heard, or smelled, or touched, or…

Initially, *huge* might be bigger than normal. In time, your image of a huge knob (629) might be a drawer handle so large that you can only see a part of it at a time. With practice, you could move it around and see it from different viewpoints. Maybe you could get inside it and roam amongst the molecules: who needs electronics to experience virtual reality? This is good, heady, creative stuff. But it is disciplined: all this variation is for a specific purpose. The further reaches of your mind are being explored. The mundane and the ordinary are being left behind.

In the early stages, you might represent *weak* as bent, the simple material condition of not having the strength to carry itself properly. You might record 738 (a weak movie) as a screen (or however you envisage 38) drooping at the edges because the frame isn't strong enough to hold it up. Later, this will evolve into an assessment of a movie as being second-rate. The impression of the film is still one of weakness, but more the feeling of being a bad movie (your opinion) than the actual sagging screen (a physical fact). Your thinking is evolving to a higher, more abstract level.

Heavy could be denoted as being suspended from a cable for support, or as a dull, uninteresting affair.

Happy might be a smile. Happy could be portrayed as movement, such as a dog—(your dog?)—wagging its tail; or as laughter…a mood, a state of mind, whatever.

Oh, that reminds me, I have never seen a happy jail (965). Come to think of it, I have never seen my yellow rain (3542) either, or have I? But an icy, black fire (0384)…naah.

A good way to practice is to play with car registration numbers while on the road and out of mental gear. Juggle license plates:

ABC 012 would be 900l2 (drop the vowel A, and you're left with "bee" and "see"—9 and 0). Now you have a choice: a hoop (9) and an icy, green tin (0012)? Or a bus (90) and a green tin (012)?

However you choose to organize your images, just be consistent.

XYZ 987 would be 700987 (the *sound* of X is a "k" and a "sss"; drop Y—you know *why;* and Z is a "zzz"—7 and 0, and 0). As usual, you decide: silver sauce (700) and a pink fake (987)? Or a case (70) and an icy, pink fake (0987)?

There are numbers everywhere: at home, in the office, outdoors, indoors, in stores…Aunt Mabel's telephone, street, and apartment…everywhere.

Play with words ; xylophone, eccentric, exaggerate, DiggedyDog…

Play with numbers. You'll become very comfortable with these wiggles-'n'-squiggles and you'll develop a really comfortable feel for the *Sound* System.

You'll look for pattern:
>   in 628 4328 (repetition of 28),
>   in 345 7652 (ascending 345 and descending 765), and
>   in 3743 (beginning and ending in 3, with a car in the middle).

You'll find meaning:
>   in 1225 you'll see Xmas Day,
>   in 0923 is Aunt Mabel's birthday, and
>   in 7863 is Dan's phone number, minus 100.

You'll use the *Sound* System, as in the following example.
>   In 795 7295 there are two bells; the first is silver, and the second is
>   weak and blue.

As you become more and more familiar with the *Sound* System, your whole mental process will become freer and more fluid. The interdependent skills of managed emotion, soaring imagination, and organized thinking will be blended within one framework.

>   New, fresh, and exciting thinks will emerge:
>   cosmothinks and astrothinks.
>   Such thinks are memorable.

23

Hallowed Be Thy Name

You and your name are your most prized possessions.

If you were shown a photograph of your old school class, whom would you look for first? Yourself, wouldn't you?

If you were watching old family movies, whom would you focus on? You would follow the action and focus on the main event: you!

If you were reminiscing with a couple of friends about old times, whose "old times" would you be talking about? Yours, of course!

In everyday conversation, whose experience do you center on? Your own, naturally.

If you were looking through a list of names, whose would you look for first? Sure, it'd be the big "U"!

In business, who wants to make a face for himself or a name for the other guy or gal? Nobody; we only set out to make a name for ourselves.

Which is your favorite restaurant? The one where the maitre d' knows you…by name!

We all need the recognition of our friends and associates. One of the quickest ways to attain this is to remember the most important word, the sweetest sound, in their world: their name. To boost another's ego and make them feel good, start by using their name. If you wish to show someone respect, to accord recognition, and to give pleasure, address that person by name.

We value our names; they are a personal treasure.

For me, the unique, quintessential *I* is encapsulated in that simple word *Robin*. If you want to attract my attention, use that special verbal label that means *me*. *Robin* is a fast track to getting my attention, and to earning my respect and liking. You attribute worth to me when you use that term. You acknowledge my individuality and honor me by saying, "I remember you. You deserve to be remembered. You are memorable." I need to be recognized, and spoken to, by name. And so do you.

Thy name is truly hallowed.

Remembering names is a most important aspect of our lives, and one of the most difficult.

There are three main reasons why this is so.

A mere sixty or seventy years ago, we would have met only a few people every day. Both person and name would probably have been very well known to us. Most likely they were locals. Contact with people was limited and comfortable. Now, in the course of an average day, many of us are exposed to more people than our grandparents were in a week. The sheer number can be mind-numbing.

Moreover, in today's global village, many names are strange, weird-sounding, and meaningless. (In fact, names are similarly derived all over the world, but they are not so simple if you do not know the language. Few of us are familiar with these ways of indicating *son of*: *Ben*Gurion, *Ze*dung, Ceaus*escu, ibn* Saud, Krzychylkie*wicz*, Mend*ez*, or Rachman*inoff*.)

As children, many of us were brought up with cautions like "Don't stare" and "It's rude to point." Usually we translated these as "Don't notice," or worse still, "Don't look". Unfortunately, most of us still follow this rigid advice. Not only do we not observe a face closely…we don't even pay attention! Because our eyes do not see, our minds have no data to interpret.

We tend to have a very weak vocabulary when it comes to faces. Until recently, we simply have not needed the words. In today's often impersonal world, it is imperative that we develop a sensitivity to faces and fine-tune our knowledge of the scores of different facial features.

We belittle, underestimate, and sell ourselves short; passively degrade ourselves; fall prey to our negative beliefs; conspire with our own stinking thinking; ensnare ourselves in false self-limiting behavior; become the victims of our own despicable self-fulfilling prophecies; convince ourselves of something both untrue and unacceptable; reinforce, with reprehensible effect, the power of negative expectation; and insult our minds, demean our intelligence, and offend our portfolio of possibilities with the lie "I cannot remember names."

As a result of this odious belief, we make no attempt to remedy the situation. We conveniently sidestep the issue. We pass the buck. We refuse to accept responsibility. Get my drift, dear reader?

This is when we do not intend to remember in the first place, anyway! Isn't that what you are being told when somebody says to you, "I never remember names"? You are being warned by that person that they have already decided "I will not remember your name!" How weird...how rude is that? How self-limiting.

All too often, this docile acceptance is converted into a matter of pride: people brag about their so-called inability! Can you imagine yourself boasting about being an inadequate parent or feeble in your career? Of course not.

Yet even you yourself might possibly have been guilty of so contemptible an attitude a little while ago, but that would have been B4...before *Yumm*. Wouldn't it!

If you intend to remember a name, it is important to be aware that you will be in one of two different situations. Either you are meeting a person for the first time, so both the face and the name are unfamiliar, or you "know" the person you are meeting, so the face is familiar but the name is...elusive? You will probably recognize the face, but you need to recall the name. Recognition and recall are different. Recognition (literally, to know again) means to identify something as familiar. Recall, on the other hand, means to bring something back to mind.

The question "Why is a face easier to remember than a name?" addresses the difference in everyday, practical terms. There are four reasons:

(1) A face is a single memory entity. A name, on the other hand, is often two unrelated items that will need to be recalled the next time you meet that person again, e.g., "Aunt Mabel, I'd like you to meet my friend of long ago, Theghn McGinty." Both Theghn and McGinty need to be borne in mind for later recall.

(2) We usually see the face (a picture), but hear the name (a word or words). Most of us remember things we see better than things we hear. Put another way, a picture (a face) is usually more memorable than words (a name).

(3) A face is a living, breathing organism, and the most expressive part of us. Our visages both show and evoke feelings, and emotions are very memorable. Seeing a face and the actual touch of shaking hands, or making some body movement, seems to be one, continuous act. Listening to, and hearing, the name seems to be something separate that is often overlooked.

(4) When you meet someone again, their face is right there in front of you as a visual reminder. You need only recognize it. But there is no reminder (visual, verbal, or any other) as to the name. There is no Oh-Zone, no "Oh, that reminds me," so the name is difficult to recall.

When you and I set out for the bathroom, we have a plan. When you and I brush our teeth, we have a tool. When you and I comb our hair, we have a system. When you and I make a cup of tea, we have a technique. When you and I get dressed, we have a method.

Yet when it comes to something as important as remembering a name, we have no plan, no tool, no technique, no system, and no method.

Makes you think, doesn't it?

Memory for names must be trained, just like any other aspect of memory. As with any skill—from working an abacus to fastening a zipper—we must know and understand, and practice with what works.

This chapter is a bird's-eye view of names and their importance. The following chapter is a worm's-eye view of specifics: bare, ragged-arsed essentials. Y'all know what I mean? Reasonable things like plans, tools, techniques, systems, and methods…just good ol' common sense.

Makes you wanna weep, don't it?

24

The Game of the Name

Life is about people, and the sweetest sound in their world is their name. Honor those you meet. Respect them. Recognize their value. Acknowledge their worth. Remember, and use, their *name.*

This is a basic skill in today's global village. Put yourself at a big advantage socially and in business by developing this inborn talent. You *do* have the ability to recollect those names, and you *can* make names memorable. Learn to remember and *use* names.

Throughout this chapter I use the inclusive pronoun "we." My intention is not to accuse you or blame you, or attribute negative qualities to you, or tell you what to do. "We" is just more personal. Please don't be offended; it's not meant personally.]

The first stage in the process of remembering names is to get set.

We need to set ourselves up mentally by starting to get out of old, bad habits we have used when we meet people: characteristics such as painfully shy, flustered, distant, overpowering, or whatever. (Please remember that causing affront is *not* what I'm about!). We should begin to focus deliberately on people in order to create an ongoing consciousness of their faces and their names. We should ask ourselves, "If I meet someone unexpectedly, will I have sufficient presence of mind to be enthusiastic and charming?" In other words, "Will I be in full control of myself?"

We must get ourselves into the habit of always being pleasantly prepared to meet people so we can be warmly involved with the introduction.

Before joining a group or gathering, we compose ourselves and relax. We make an opportunity to actually stop, or maybe just pause, and take a long, deep breath in order to get quiet and composed. We deliberately try to get ourselves into a confident frame of mind—ready to succeed. Positive expectancy is very powerful. If we believe that our memory is going to get better, we will notice an immediate improvement.

"Who is most likely to be there: family, friends, business associates, people I have not met before but might have heard about, complete strangers? Who might I meet?"

"Whoever they are, I *will* remember, and use, their names."

The second stage in the process of remembering names is to get the name.

We must have a thing in mind before we can forget it. Frequently we say we "forgot" something. What we should say is that we never actually got it in the first place. This failure to deliberately direct our thinking is the most common reason for "forgetting" the names of people we meet.

Make it your intention, consistently and persistently, to pay...with attention.

On meeting someone, most of us look at the other person. But we see only with our eyes, not with our mind. We don't look at that other person in order to observe; we are thinking about our reply. We aren't taking note; we're preparing to speak. As we shake hands and our new acquaintance tells us his or her name, what is going through our mind?

"Big, strong hands. Wet, clammy grip. Where'd he get that tie? It's costume jewelry. Nice, very nice. Oh look, there's Jane. Funny glasses. Is that a hairpiece? Great perfume. Is he important to us? Is she attracted to me? How am I coming across? Everyone's looking at me! God, I'm gorgeous! I need a dazzling remark to impress. How does my hair look? How can I get control? Is there spinach on my teeth? Is my zipper undone?"

"What was that name? Damn it, I've forgotten...already!"

When we are focusing on the impression we are making on others, we are actually only thinking of ourselves. Instead, we should develop a sincere and genuine interest in other people, and they will automatically like us. Interest is a key ingredient for effective remembering.

Even when we are paying attention, we may not catch the person's name if it is spoken too fast, too quietly, or too indistinctly. When this happens, we simply stop and ask them to repeat their name. People will be flattered because we are showing a genuine interest in them. They will probably warm to us instantly. This is so obvious, but done so seldom. Furthermore, such a question can be an effective "ice-breaker": it melts the initial tension when meeting new people.

However we do it, we must get the name. This is essential. There will be an immediate improvement in our ability to recall names. However we do it, we *must* get the name.

The third stage in the process of remembering names is to make the name meaningful.

A meaningful name is memorable. It is more difficult to recall a name if it has no meaning. (Remember the solitary word *little*? All by itself, *little* made no sense; it had no context, no reference points. However, it had meaning when associated with *red book*. *Little* alone is not memorable. *Little red book* is memorable.)

Names fall into three categories:

Many names are already meaningful in themselves, and so suggest immediate (mental) pictures. For instance:

adjectives:	Long, Short, Strong
animals:	Hogg, Lamb, Wolff
birds:	Falcon, Jay, Sparrow
brand names:	Bentley, Hershey, Seagram
colors:	Black, Green, White
companies:	Harrod, McDonald, Sears
famous people:	Barnard, Churchill, Mandela
metals:	Gold, Silver, Steele
months:	March, April, May
names of cities:	London, Washington, Sydney
countries:	Holland, Ireland, Wales
peoples:	French, Irish, Scott
occupations:	Barber, Cook, Cooper
plants:	Lily, Oaks, Rose
precious stones:	Diamond, Pearl, Ruby
things:	Ball, Bell, Hammer, and so on.

Other names have no meaning in themselves, but may make sense to us personally by association with a name or a word we already know.

Let's suppose that we meet Louis, the Ziquubu family, Athanasia, and Lola.

Suppose we already know a Louise. We will resort to the Oh-Zone: create some hook or link associating (this "new," unfamiliar) Louis with (the "old," familiar) Louise. Next time we see Louis, Louise will spring to mind as if by magic, and we will have her name.

Ziquubu sounds very strange. But Charles Sibuku is a great friend. Ziquubu sounds very similar to the familiar Sibuku. So to remember the name Ziquubu is easy for us.

Athanasia is a word similar to euthanasia. We could create very strong (emotional) links with this one.

Lola is a word pretty close to the other half of Coca. Another connection could be the shapely bottle of that world-famous brand and a voluptuous Lola.

Such a process might seem ridiculous to our educated, analytical minds. But to our natural, childlike imagination—the limbic part of us, maybe—this is a game, and fun. We have nothing to lose, so let's try it. It works.

Many names have no meaning whatsoever. To give them meaning, we replace them with a meaningful word that we can picture. To illustrate, I picked the following names out of the telephone directory, at random.

Baderdien might be remembered as the food and beverage manager—the head (the dean) of food (the larder). This replaces a syllable with a similar sound, while also turning the name back to front: "dean larder" for Baderdien.

Dagbo may be replaced by thinking of dat bow—pidgin English for "that bow."

Farnell could be made memorable by "hearing" a distant knell: a bell ringing some way away. I know this is sound, not sight; but with the mixing and matching of the senses, we are using the mind's ingenuity to help us fix a name in our memory. Remember the *me* of *me*mory expansion and *m*ind extension?

Othmann sounds similar to "other man"—whoever we think he is.

Ruff could be connected to the sense of touch: "rough."

Sauer is pronounced "sour" and has a sharp, biting taste.

Schwartz is a name similar to the German word for black, so that color might be the basis for a memorable mental invention.

Trilan sounds like three lambs. That's easy to see in the mind's eye. Why not say it to ourselves, repeatedly as well, using our mind's ear?

Unga could be replaced with the sound-alike and rhyming (sensation of) hunger.

We should use as many senses as possible to try and make the name not just memorable, but unforgettable. We want to give it a unique personality; to make that name an actual, living experience. Productive inventiveness follows neither logic or reason. Creativity thrives on being spontaneous. Our imagination is unique to us. Let's be free to let go, and play. Be effective.

We will come across the occasional name that we are not able to make completely meaningful in the time available. But merely having tried to do so will help us remember it. The simple fact of having focused our attention, for the briefest period of time, supports memory. As soon as we have time, we return to that name and create a mental reminder. If necessary, we ask somebody in order to jog our memory.

Learning any new skill takes time and effort—what we call practice. This exercise returns immense value for the time and effort spent. Not only will we be extending our ability to remember names, but we will also be revitalizing that magical faculty called our creative imagination. We ought to be consistent and persistent. With repetition, the whole process will become quicker and easier. Gradually we will bring into being a new way of thinking, a fresh habit, an appropriate attitude.

The fourth stage in the process of remembering names is to focus on a feature.

We need to note at least one distinctive feature of the person. This would most likely be a prominent part of the face. But other parts of the body, as well as physical traits, are also very compelling. Next time we meet this individual, the distinctive feature should immediately attract our attention and jog our memory.

The purpose of focusing on and observing the face is to find something outstanding that will help us recognize it. Few of us are practiced at this. As a result, it is difficult to find something really noteworthy. All faces have the same basic features: two eyes, a nose, and a mouth, with an ear on each side for good measure. Because we observe so little, our vocabulary for describing a face is seriously limited, and often inadequate. We have not needed the words. In fact, faces have many distinguishing characteristics—literally hundreds—but we must train ourselves to look for and see them. We need to do more that just see with our eyes.

We should observe actively, with our minds! While watching TV, we can do a valuable exercise: Use the remote to turn the sound all the way down and observe the faces. Maybe focus on features, individual characteristics, and people's traits, as well. We can do this while the commercials are on, or between programs. Watch intently; pay...with attention!

No time or money is involved, just a little nice 'n' easy *me*. This ongoing training can be of phenomenal benefit, for we can develop our consciousness of physical appearance.

We really do need to enlarge our range of descriptive words. Below are some that describe a variety of facial features. The list is extensive and meant for reference only. Browse through it.

Size of the head:
large, medium, small

Head and face, full-on:
square, rectangular, round, oval, triangular with the base at the chin and the point at the scalp, triangular with the base at the scalp and the point at the chin, broad, narrow, big-boned, fine-boned

Head from the side:
square, rectangular, oval, broad, narrow, round, egg-shaped, flat at the front, flat on top, flat at the back, domed at the back, face angled with jutting chin and slanted forehead, face angled with receding chin, prominent forehead, face concave, face convex

Hair:
Texture: fine, wavy, straight, permed, frizzy, lank, thick, shiny
Style, men: parted, full, receding, bald, cropped, medium-length
Style, women: curly, short, long, plaited, pony-tailed, bobbed, pinned-up, loose
Color: black, light or dark brown, light or dark blonde, red, ginger, gray, white; artificial streaks, tints, and highlights

Beware of hair; it can change dramatically from one meeting to the next. Moustaches and beards can come and go. Hair that is stringy and oily today will probably be clean and shiny tomorrow. Styles, lengths, and colors can be altered.

Forehead:
high, wide, narrow between hairline and eyebrows, narrow between temples, lined (wrinkled) vertically, lined horizontally, smooth

Eyebrows:
thick, thin, long, short, meeting at the middle, spaced apart, arched, flat, winged, bushy, tapered (gradually narrowing)

Eyelashes:
long, curly, short, straight, thick, thin

Eyes:
large, small, protruding, deep-set, close together, spaced apart, slanted outward, slanted inward, almond-shaped, cross-eyed (squint), color of the pupil, iris completely visible, iris covered partly by upper and/or lower lid

Eyelids:
puffy above and/or below the eye, large, small, smooth, wrinkled, firm, crow's feet (lines at the corners)

Nose:
from the front: large, small, narrow, medium, wide, crooked.
from the side: straight, flat, pointed, blunt, snub, upturned (pug),Roman/aquiline (hooked like an eagle's beak), Greek (forming straight line with forehead), concave, convex

Nostrils:
straight, curved down, flaring, wide, narrow, hairy, pinched

Ears:
large, small, gnarled, smooth, round, oblong, triangular, flat against the head, protruding, cauliflower, hairy, large-lobed, no lobes, uneven, set high or low on the head
Ears, especially men's, are as individual as fingerprints.

Cheeks:
sunken, bony, full

Cheekbones:
high, prominent, obscured

Lips:
long upper lip, short upper lip, lip overlap, small, thick, wide, thin, upturned, downturned, Cupid's bow (arched), well-shaped, ill-defined

Mouth:
upper lip thickens, lower lip thickens, lip overlap, width, lines from the nostrils to the corners of the mouth
Mouths are very expressive. They tell us a lot about personality and mood.

Teeth:
regular, irregular, gaps, discolored, missing, white, capped, large, small, buck, pointed, square

Chin/jaw:
from front: long, short, pointed, square, round, double (or multiple), cleft, dimpled from side: jutting, straight, double (or multiple), receding

Skin and coloring:
smooth, rough, dark, fair, rosy, pale, sallow, blemished/marked/pitted, oily, dry, blotchy, doughy, wrinkled, furrowed, freckled, tanned, transparent

Other features:
scars, warts, growths, birthmarks, smile lines.

Physical characteristics are often very striking. There may be peculiarities of walk—a limp, a shuffle, a confident stride, or a readily noticeable bearing or posture: imposing, stooped, shoulders back and chest out, head held at an angle.

Other useful features might be a particular smile or a distinctive laugh, peculiar gestures and mannerisms, a twitch or nervous tic, unusual height or shortness, strange physique, disabilities, or disfigurements.

Beware of features that may change: length, color, and style of hair; presence or absence of a beard or moustache and glasses; style and shade of glasses; anything worn, such as jewelry and clothing (including coloring and style of makeup).

A voice is a second face. Voices, like faces, are all different and quite distinctive—ask any experienced telephone user. I find that I associate certain voice types with pictures:

authoritative—the chairman, in full cry
brassy (loud and vulgar)—a huge van's air-brakes on a steep hill
crackling—popcorn being made
deep and husky—a smoker of Churchill cigars
gravelly (harsh and grating)—leather soles walking on coarse sand
high-pitched—a group of excited girls
hoarse—guess?
monotonous—a long, boring journey
rough—coarse sandpaper grating on glass
slow—a peak-performance racing tortoise
smooth—flowing golden syrup
squeaky—a rusted farm gate when opening
staccato—a little boy playing with his toy machine-gun
undulating—a small boat on a gentle sea swell
weak—an exhausted marathon runner.

Speech peculiarities are useful: a lisp, where the **s** and **z** sounds are pronounced **th**; repetition of certain words or phrases (might be just a passing phase); or mispronunciation and incorrect language usage. Speaking style and content could be amusing, articulate, clipped, flowery and pompous, informed and interesting, monotonous, or monosyllabic.

Accents have powerful memory value. To help me remember a person's accent, I picture the symbols of various countries, such as Big Ben, the Brandenburg Gate, Crocodile Dundee, the Eiffel Tower, Mount Fuji, the Statue of Liberty, and so on. I link the symbol to the name. Develop your awareness of voices, speech, and accents on the radio, on TV, among colleagues at work, friends, family, and people at parties.

Facial expression is more abstract, but carefully studying the whole face can strengthen our memory. Making a judgment about a person's character or personality (alert, animated, deadpan, dour, honest, intelligent, kind, sour, warm…) improves the chances that we will remember the name even more than an awareness of physical characteristics does. This is because we make ourselves conscious of the whole person.

We do tend to remember faces that are distinctive and striking better than those that are not. Appealing Hollywood stars are more memorable than the average supermarket shopper. We are also better at recognizing faces from our own race. With intention and practice, these deficiencies can be remedied.

These assessments help to pinpoint our attention. They intensify our observation, creating an automatic interest in the other being. Nothing is interesting if we are not interested. In addition, we have obliged ourselves to focus on that other person. We cannot be thinking of ourselves!

The fifth stage in the process of remembering names is to glue the two (meaning and feature) together.

After we have made the name meaningful and noted a distinctive feature (probably facial) of the person, we should form a conscious association between the two. This, again, is the Oh-Zone and "Oh, that reminds me."

The mind is a vast system of interconnections. The next time we see that individual the name will automatically spring to tongue-tip, if the pictures and the way they interact are sufficiently strong.

The sixth stage in the process of remembering names is to review.

An excellent way to start is to address the person we are meeting by name. We all know this, but not many of us do it. Not only is there the obvious benefit of according recognition and respect, but repetition also helps to consolidate the name in our mind. Saying something out loud is a powerful aid to learning, because it involves more effort.

Review the name (literally "look at it again") after a few minutes, and then again several minutes later. Use our mind's ear by actually saying the name—at least to ourselves. Repeat it a couple of times. Spell it, as well as we're able. We see it. We link it with something similar or familiar. We create as many hooks and knots as possible to tie it into memory. *Peat, peat, and more peat* is the mother of learning, which is why reviewing is so vitally important.

Next time we're with people, we'll try this exercise: When appropriate, we'll take a few seconds and (mentally) withdraw. In our mind's eye, we'll work our way around the table, along the bar, over the group, through the rows, and around the room.

We'll recreate the gathering. Using our imagination, we'll recall each person and their name: "Who's on my left? What does he look like; can I picture his face?" No? Steal a quick peek. "Of course, I'd missed that whiney voice/tiny mouth/shiny pate. And what's the name? I remember: It rhymes with the name of my archaeologist cousin who works in a canyon. Banyon, Danyon, Damyon…that's it, Damyon. Who's next to him? Big ears…ringing…a bell…something to do with a bell, and a question…Got it: Isobel. Beside her is the man with the fixed stare: Glare, Nare…I asked him how he spelled such an unusual name—Nair. I can see the woman across the table from him. She talks a load of drivel: Kniffel, Irma Kniffel. I can't envisage who's on her right; I'll take a look…oh yes, thin lips…cruel…Tartars…Crimea…Florence Nightingale…That's her: Knight, Jane Knight."

And so memory and creative imagination sweep invincibly on, a tireless two-some—illogical, unreasonable, way-out, crude, disrespectful, honest, childlike, freewheeling, and fun…and wonderfully effective.

These six steps can be summarized as:

get set; **get** (the name); **M2** (**m**ake it **m**eaningful); **F2** (**f**ocus on a **f**eature); **glue** (meaning and feature); and **review**.

We need to follow these guidelines and apply these principles—use them, practice them, exercise 'em, do 'em, practice, apply…always *me*.

Watch the improvement in ourselves; acknowledge the improvement to ourselves.

To remember people and their names
we should
get set
get
M2
F2
glue
review

25

To Get Older Is to Become Wiser

As we grow older, new possibilities unfold. Our store of learning builds up and the sum of what actually happens to us accumulates.

Lived knowledge and learned knowledge blend. This network of knowing grows endlessly. What we know spreads and fuses with other stuff. Stored information increasingly interconnects. Awareness unfurls. Our consciousness unravels and broadens. As we evolve as a person, our sensitivity becomes finer and more subtle. As we understand more, we become progressively more insightful. We grow as individuals. "I" becomes a progressively more informed and enlightened "I." Our aging mind is capable of lifelong growth.

Our accumulated wisdom and experience can reward us with a much richer inner being than ever before. Surely this ongoing process of unrolling under-standing—U2—must contain the meaning of our lives? As youth ages, it pro-gressively discards ignorance. As the years roll on, you and I gain wisdom. We learn who we are and why we are here. This strengthens us; we can contribute more, and so receive more. And so the cycle of fulfilling our purpose grows and reinforces itself. All this is built on being able to understand more and to remember effectively.

Memory is of universal interest. Nearly every person I meet has an opinion on the subject. Usually I am simply told, "I'm useless at remembering names" or "I can't remember like I used to—and the older I get, the worse it gets." How to remember names is dealt with in the previous two chapters. This chapter is about the second topic: memory and advancing years. However, there are two areas I do not cover.

First, I don't talk about memory and old age. Rather, I look at memory in the context of merely getting older. There is a discipline that deals with the study of aging and the problems faced by elderly people. Gerontology does not form part of this book.

Second, I don't consider a memory that is defective. This means that I assume there is no brain damage or deterioration. The general effect of physical aging is to reduce the support the body gives the brain. Changes in the (material) state of the brain, such as a reduced blood supply, can have profound effects upon mental functioning. Furthermore, in a mind that is disturbed, memory is unlikely to work as it should.

As this could not be a medical book, a person who is either physiologically or psychologically impaired is outside its possible scope. But body and mind are interdependent. In order to perform at peak efficiency, both need to be healthy. Alter one, and the other will be affected. Nothing can exist alone.

As you know, this *little red book* is about renewing mental vitality and re-energizing mighty mind,; about further developing the astonishing capacities that you have always possessed; about continuously striving to make the most of what you have. Anyone, at any age, can improve through greater consciousness and understanding of memory and by using tools and techniques.

There are two main reasons why memory might appear to get weaker as we get older: cultural beliefs and social attitudes, and our own thinking.

Culture is the sum of the ideas and customs, and the art and science, that are common to and unite a society. Culture defines the basic value system—what is seen as right and wrong, and what is important to the group. We can be very shallow, because we are an eye-minded society. What we see, is. Appearances are all-important; by glancing at the surface we believe we can judge the whole. By scanning the cover of a book, we reckon we can assess the contents…All that glistens *is* gold. However, we do have other guiding tenets.

Our society also reveres sensory pleasure. This is expressed through our obsession with youth, physical beauty, and boundless energy. Efficiency is most often associated with activity. If you look busy—are seen to be strenuously involved—you'll usually be given the benefit of the doubt. If you're rushing, hectic and frenetic, it's assumed that you're being effective. We have become addicted to a number of power habits. There's the "do, do, do" with sound and movement—the former loud, the latter vigorous; the "go, go, go"—personally pulsating through every high-impact, super-strength nanosecond; and the "come, come, come"—to be young and promiscuous is fashionable; it's in.

Beautiful young people are a creation of nature. We admire the bold, the brave, and the young. This admiration is good, but it can be overdone. Our cultural reverence for youth and action does have a very negative effect in our advancing years. Have you noticed how some people, as they get older, seem to feel progressively less relevant and involved? They appear to think that they are being reduced to mere observer status. They simply watch life's passing parade. They allow themselves to believe that they are marginalized, no longer contributing meaningfully; that they have passed some self-evident sell-by date. Beautiful old people must create themselves.

Unless we are careful, with the passing of the years our will to lead and make things happen seems to weaken, and eventually it becomes a desire to hand over control of our lives. The effect is cumulative: When the urge to action is seemingly thwarted, it atrophies into a wish to be taken care of. Too many people surrender their independence to the domination of others, who are, of course, the energetic and the assertive.

Responsibility for their own lives is passively given up to someone who "knows better." These folk cease trying to be proactive. Others are allowed to take control. Those who have voluntarily relinquished their minds to "out there" tend to seek one another out. If you put yourself in the company of the lame, you will soon be lame yourself. And so the trend of passively yielding and dropping out grows and reinforces itself.

Too many of us trap ourselves in this false "thinking." Of course it is right for youth to be active and energetic. And yes, the benign and experienced minds of older people should think and plan and guide and lead. But youth is not primarily a time of life; it is a state of mind. Few grow old by living a number of years. They grow old because they allow the days to run into each other, so that little seems to separate Monday from Thursday, March from October, 1986 from 1996. Life is endured, not lived. Yesterday is not really different from today. Hopefully there won't be any surprises, so tomorrow will be more of the same.

There is tedium, year in and year out. On the principle of "use it or lose it," our minds lose their acuity. Our sharpness succumbs to disuse, and it atrophies. Most grow old by losing their youthful enthusiasm and by relinquishing their natural curiosity. They grow old because they have abandoned their unrealized dreams and jettisoned their unfulfilled hopes. They don't challenge themselves mentally any more. Through neglect, they live increasingly in the past because they have no plans for tomorrow. Boredom and inertia are viruses. Don't catch them.

Most of our behavior is automatic, driven by habit. We call these habits of thought "attitudes." You can't age thought; you can't age spirit. Intellect and creativity don't slow down with the years. Being young is not merely a question of chronology; it is largely a set of self-enhancing beliefs and a pattern of "positive" expectations. It is the youthful focus on moving forward. The aged, even fifteen-year-old antiques, peer continuously over their shoulder. At first, they soak themselves in the past, and soon they are drowning in yesterday. Age is mostly attitude.

Some of us shirk our responsibility to ourselves. We start by invoking a profound truism: "I am getting older." "How convenient," we say to ourselves. "This is easy. I have a ready-made excuse: I can always blame…time!"

But look how these people set themselves up for failure. Using age as an excuse, they have primed themselves to "not remember" ("I'm not getting any younger, you know"). They expect to forget ("I won't remember"). Without thinking, they have given their mind a simple instruction: "Don't remember!" Mind obeys; that is its nature. Thoughtlessly, they accuse and abuse a vital aspect of their very identity: "It's my useless memory." Finally, time becomes the scapegoat: "It's age, you know." But it isn't age, you know…

Life is an ongoing process of growth and development. As our minds mature, preferences shift. Over the years, we think and remember differently—as we evolve, out of habit, as a matter of course, with age and experience. Some memory skills fade; others develop. With age, we know more. We increasingly see the connections between diverse bits of knowing. Our knowledge becomes better integrated. We have tremendous growth in acumen and good judgment. Supporting detail is secondary, for we see life more as a whole.

In age we understand. Unconsciously, we look for wider interpretation, deeper meaning, and broader significance. We cross-refer, have insights, make connections, draw inferences, make judgments, form opinions, and integrate into a broader context. We are more mature, and wiser. At sixty, I must be a more developed mind than I was at sixteen. I focus on the advantages of increasing insight and keener judgment. For heaven's sake, this is exactly as it should be.

In youth we learn. A young person craves morsels of knowledge and scraps of information. She thrives on rote recall and remembering events "exactly as they happened." She describes people and reconstructs circumstances; there is no interpretation. Strings of facts and figures—names, events, telephone numbers—are grist to her mental mill. She has to establish her own database. She has to stock her personal library.

She and I view information through different eyes. We have different priorities. Why, then, would I compare myself with her? At this stage, I do not want to distract myself with detail. I know that I can always get the minutiae of Aunt Mabel's address and telephone number.

Yet so many of us try to compete with these eager young brains focused on the bald specifics. At a very shallow level, we vie with them. And we find ourselves lacking, so we make a self-damning inference: "She must be better; therefore, I must be slipping." The noose tightens and we fall into that age-old trap: "My memory is failing; it must be…age." And so the downward spiral of negative expectation starts to wreak its devastating havoc.

We have all seen older people who lose interest in "out there." (In fairness, I have seen fifteen-year-olds who have already made up their minds; they do not want the facts either.) The world of these older folk becomes progressively smaller. Their thinking is rooted in "when I" and "the way it used to be." Much of the day is spent in head-shaking and disapproval, and comparing the present with "the good old days." Such folk unconsciously withdraw from the present moment to seek refuge in the past, which they remember as secure and nonthreatening. Yesterday things were different; "then" was better.

With this mind-set they deny the future. With this attitude they refuse to contemplate tomorrow. Their lives are commanded by routine and habit. They cling to old times, and so they have lost their adaptability. Rigidity of thoughts and feelings tenses both mind and body. There is no place for new ideas and novel thoughts. They feel that as they age they have to give up certain things.

Could it be that they grow old *because* they give up certain things? Let me put it another way. You have probably heard the expression that you can't teach an old dog new tricks. But there is another saying that is less well-known: The quickest way to become an old dog is to quit learning new tricks. Many choose to exist passively, by rote. This is not right.

We should live actively by design, and by ongoing learning. The times are changing, and we must change with them. Mankind was born to learn. In the context of *Yumm,* could learning be just another word for changing? Your ability to change and adapt will keep you young. Be eager, excited, and open to new ideas, new places, new people, and fresh thinking.

Our business in life is not to get ahead of others, but to get ahead of ourselves; to break our own records; to outstrip our yesterday with our achievements today. Then we need to live today as best we can, in preparation for a better tomorrow. We live better when we have something to live for.

We all have a faculty that enables us to look backward to the past, to relate that past to the present, and to use it to determine our future. The faculty of remembering preserves the continuity of life's experience. Expect the best of your memory. Be nostalgic—cherish your memories, but live in the present. Yesterday is gone; what have you learned from it? Thrive in Now. Get excited about tomorrow; anticipate and plan. What will you do in it? Question, enquire, ask, probe. It is never too late.

Keep yourself physically fit. Avoid spending too much time in lazy ways, such as watching TV. Your body needs to be used; it demands plenty of movement. Lack of activity feeds on itself—the less you do, the less you will want to do. Keep yourself mentally fit. Stimulate and challenge your mind. Improve yourself. Develop one of your inborn capacities. Learn a skill.

Yumm has caused you to think about memory—what it is and why it is essential in your life. You are more conscious. Surely you are beginning to suspect that your memory is potentially unlimited, aren't you? You are beginning to feel this to the core of your soul, to the essence of your being. You are starting to believe in the power of your mind. You are unplugging from your "old" thinking and tuning in to a new belief system. You are already expecting to remember more effectively, despite your......er, age.

But expectation is a two-edged sword. Thoughts (and their offspring, words) are mighty forces. Our species invented language to give voice to our thinking. Remember Theghn and his hapless band? This means that words can be strong influences for enervating us, as well as for invigorating us. Sometimes we do not act as effectively as we would like. How often have you heard people express their dissatisfaction at their own poor performance? Combining their scorn at themselves with a lack of knowledge and consciousness, they focus on the negative. They defeat themselves. For memory, this is like saying, "I won't remember!" But I'm not going down that road again.

Why not improve your faculty of remembering? It's a whole-brain endeavor. It *is* you. Having learned the tools and techniques, trust in and have fun with your pals. Make the effort to put them into practice. Train with *me* and *peat, peat, and more peat.*

It is universally agreed that those who are mentally and socially active have clearer minds in every way than those who are passive, withdrawn, and inactive. Similarly, enthusiasm, flexibility, curiosity, and a genuine interest in others all have a strong and positive influence on mental acuity, memory, and quality of life.

As Bob Dylan sang,
"If you ain't busy livin',
you're busy dyin.'"

26

When Mind Is Conspicuous
By Its Absence

There are hundreds of examples of so-called "'absentmindedness."

Do you know anyone who

•Forgets where they have parked the car?

•Misplaces their keys, their pen, their glasses?

•Opens the fridge instead of turning the kettle on?

•Has walked into another room and not known why?

•Has left the handbrake off when they have parked their car?

•Seldom remembers to pass on that message from Aunt Mabel?

•Can't remember whether or not they have switched off the lights?

•Is never sure as to whether they have turned off the stove or locked the front door?

•Fails to mail that letter to Aunt Mabel, buy her that red rose, or e-mail her Aunt Harriet?

Absentmindedness is a literal term. We allow our mind to be somewhere else; we let it be absent. Later we feel that we really needed it with us. We tried to shoplift—to acquire the goods without paying. Since there was no presence of mind, we bilked. We did not pay...with attention. Guess who *used* to be blamed?

But that was B4...before *Yumm*, wasn't it?

Let me quote from *The Game of the Name*: "We must have a thing in mind before we can forget it. Frequently we say we 'forgot' something. What we should say is that we never actually got it in the first place. This failure to deliberately direct our thinking is the most common reason for 'forgetting.'"

Absentmindedness is about inattention, not memory. The lights were on, but nobody was at home. We tried to beat the system and short-circuit the process. But there is no free lunch.

At first, when you unlocked your front door and walked into your home, you used to ask yourself the same question: "Where shall I put my keys?" After a while, your response became increasingly routine: "The same place as you normally put them." In time, this behavior became automatic. With unthinking repetition, you just put them in the usual place. As a matter of habit—unconsciously—you simply hung them on the key rack.

At the same time as you put those keys down, you could also be walking, scratching your nose (both low-level activities), sensing anything different and possibly threatening in your home (a higher level), and contemplating the importance of memory (very high level). This ability to function effectively on different levels is fundamental to your human genius.

All these different activities, both physical and mental, you have had to learn—individually, little by little, by understanding, with practice, through trial and much error, over time, and from experience. You were not born with this knowledge. As you have grown older, you have become wiser. Not only have you learned to do more things, with increasing levels of competence for each thing, but you have also learned to do these various things simultaneously. You can perform many jobs at once.

Your capacity to multi-task is remarkable and serves a vital function: Mind and body are freed to get on with more important things. Our minds are meant to learn, practice, and constantly improve. As we achieve higher levels of competence, we increasingly store lower levels as habit. More and more of our behavior becomes automatic, and thereby unconscious. This is the way we have evolved.

The little things that we do continually are just not important enough to occupy our minds. We can act mechanically without giving a thought to what we are doing. This is the way it should be. But unfortunately, conscious thought is also often absent at those outer fringes that toggle between conscious deliberate behavior and mindless automatic behavior.

Absentmindedness is a price we pay for being able to carry out so many complex activities with only a small investment of conscious attention. Usually, the trivial consequences are not serious. But when your absent mind is an irritant, you owe it to yourself—and probably at least one other—to do something about it.

Do the effects of your absentmindedness worry you? Do they concern you enough for you to admit there is a problem? Do you want to get rid of this nuisance? Are you prepared to pay the price? This is not the marketplace; dollars, deutschmarks, or doddle nuts are not legal tender. You must pay…with attention. You must make it your intention to pay with attention. That will solve the problem.

Failure to pay attention is the cause of absentmindedness. There are three reasons why your mental focus was elsewhere. You were either distracted, preoccupied, or not sufficiently organized. Here are some examples.

Distraction: As you unlocked the front door, the phone rang. You rushed into the house to answer it. Without thinking, you put the keys down. You "forgot" that you had dropped them on the back of the chair, and they were eventually found behind the cushion. The telephone was not at fault. As you entered the house, you were distracted;

Preoccupation: As you unlocked the front door and entered the house, you were deep in thought about that call to Aunt Mabel. Without thinking, you put the keys down. You "forgot" that you had dropped them on the back of the chair, and they were eventually found behind the cushion. Aunt Mabel was not to blame. As you entered the house, you were preoccupied.

Lack of personal organization: As you unlocked the front door and entered the house, you found yourself in a familiar, comfortable environment. You felt at home. Since nothing grabbed your attention, you carried on mindlessly. Without thinking, you continued with automatic and routine behavior. Out of habit, unconsciously, you put the keys down. This time, you dropped them on the back of the chair, and they were eventually found behind the cushion. The previous time you'd dropped them in a cup on the shelf. The time before that you'd left them in a kitchen cupboard, and before that in a pocket, in the CD holder…

You need to establish a specific place to put those keys. The real cause of all the annoyance is that you are not sufficiently organized. There are measures you can take. You can, of course, put those keys anywhere you choose, but do it deliberately. Otherwise, establish one particular place to put them. Why not put up a key rack? But you would still have to remember to use it.

When all is said and done, it's all, umm…just a thought. So be wise—use tools and techniques, have a method, make a plan. *Make it your intention to pay…with attention…consistently and persistently.*

Bear in mind that the master key
to overcoming absentmindedness is
trusting in and having fun with your pals.

27

The *Wise Ones* Use Tools

A tool is something we humans employ to make life easier or better, preferably both. *Yumm* is a tool. The book itself should appeal to our senses; it should look and feel good. But more important, the *little red book* must be useful, because it is dedicated to helping you improve your memory.

People today use more gadgets than ever. With tools, we are at the pinnacle of known intelligent life. Implements and machines, utensils and appliances surround us. At the moment, you probably have shoes on your feet and are sitting in a chair. *Yumm* was on a shelf or lying on a table. Shoes, a chair, a shelf, and a table are devices to make your life both easier and better. They are practical, utilitarian tools—things in the physical world of matter.

To this day, our mind is our primary weapon. We think before we act. We have also developed the ability to remember what we did and what has happened to us, and to learn from that experience. We can imagine beyond what is actually happening to us and we can conceive of and deliberately create our own future. These limitless capacities have catapulted us vastly farther than any other species. They have made us *Homo sapiens sapiens*: the Wise Ones.

To function efficiently, mind also needs tools, which are the techniques and methods for a formless, dimensionless world. Mind has developed through trial and error. As a result of this fumbling evolution, our minds are a syndicate of systems and circuits; a blend of primitive and progressive; a mix of thoughts and feelings, ideas and emotions.

At birth we are given a brain as a gift. Its offspring, mind, has to be developed. There is no cost to us, so we simply take our mental processes for granted. We tend to grossly undervalue these ultimate assets, which are awesome in their complexity. Furthermore, this wondrous child comes without a training manual or an instruction booklet. There are few guidebooks on mind. There are no maps of the mental terrain. The brochures are scarce, and the catalogs are often incomprehensible. We must design and use our own unique mental tools.

There is a good chance that a pair of glasses is perched on your nose right now. That is a device to promote better vision—a tool to help you see better. The better you see, the more raw data your brain has to translate, and so the greater the potential consciousness of your mind. And your own unfolding under-standing—U2—is what your life is all about. Sight is only one of many senses.

But what about an apparatus to strengthen your mind's eye? Do you have any utensils for your infinitely rich internal world? Do you have any tools to help you mentally?

Yumm is about what is, or can be, consciously remembered. But what tools do you use to help your memory, what devices to assist recall, what implements to bring information back to mind? What machinery is in place to support effec-tive remembering?

Before *Yumm,* did you use any systems, any methods, any techniques? Did you have any sort of plan?

28

And These Are the Tools
The *Wise Ones* Use

Near the beginning of *Yumm,* you met Naauw A'Daze. She issued herself a challenge (to sit at the tip of the great boulder) and set herself an objective (to gain the best view of the valley). In quick succession, she attained both of those aims. Her intention underpinned successful effort. Instantly, she felt elated. She had enhanced her own self-confidence. And she had reinforced the maxim by which she always tried to live: *If it's to be, it is up to me.*

Naauw is a metaphor for you, dear reader. Are you prepared to challenge yourself; to begin exploring the furthermost fringes of your magnificent memory? Will you develop an unshakeable attitude of positive excitement toward expanding your mind? Do you really intend to develop a superb memory in those areas that you really care about and sincerely desire to improve? Will you set yourself an objective: to understand the principles of the *Sound* System, to learn, and to practice? It *is* true: it *is* up to you.

Pals is about methodical and systematic remembering. All memory is based on reminders (literally, to bring back to mind; to re-mind.) One thing reminds you of the next in an endless process of association and linking. To remember effectively, record data in as many sensory ways as possible, and blend those senses with strong emotion in order to create complete living experiences in mind. These are not just memorable; they are also unforgettable. This is the essence of *your pals*: *Have fun with them and trust them.*

Impressions are received by the senses. Mind interprets—makes sense of—these meaningless impulses. Mere data is converted into information. Our task is to secure this material in mind, but that is only half the job. To be of value, the material must also be found again. So we deliberately use hooks, make links, and create connections in order to recover the information again. In other words—to remember it.

Here are some of the techniques that you can use to help you lock information into your mind, and the keys to release it again.

*Use **abbreviations**.*

R N stands for Reflective Neanderthal, Royal Navy, and Registered Nurse;

TLC is thinking, learning, and creating; whereas tlc is tender, loving care;

SST is supersonic travel, as well as sight, sound, and touch—or is it seeing, smelling, and tasting?

What are the three traditional "Rs"?

What do M2 and F2 stand for? What's the rest of the sequence, and what does it all actually mean in terms of practical, everyday behavior?

*Use **acronyms**.*

Acronyms are words made up of the first letters of the items to be remembered, such as:

GUTs, pals, *Yumm* and *me,* rut and U2…LO and behold!

Could *umm* stand for universal mighty mind?

If you can't recall the GUTs of memory right now, you'll find them in the cage. Would that be on page…76? By using the *Sound* System as a skeleton, you could remember vast amounts of information.

Imagine if you were trying to remember page numbers, pictures, and layouts and contents of books, magazines, or newspapers?

What is the name of the person mentioned on page 82? So as to remember next time, have him on the phone.

In your mind's eye, see Yest A'Daze linked to a tin. On what page does he figure?

Naauw (toad) and Nero (boat) are on what page?

Use **acrostics.**

In an acrostic, the first letters of the items to be remembered make up the first letters of a sentence. What about: Reason understands thinking? And something about cud-chewers?

Use **alliteration.**

This is the use of the same letter at the beginning of each word, as in

Missing method might mean meager memory;

Hoots and howls, or grunts, groans, and gestures;

Red is a color, like russet, rufous, and ruby.

Associate.

A rut is also a dreary and unchanging routine, and then there's something about an annual event…?

A certain Mr. Collins told us about ruts and…petitions, was it?

Does the *little red book* remind you of another publication?

In *Yumm,* I have used the *Sound* System. Can you think of any other sound systems…apart from Philips or Pioneer? By the way, *trusting in and having fun with your pals* is also a sound and reliable system;

What do you associate with Walt Disney World and the Kennedy Space Center…Would you repeat that?

Oh, that reminds me—R N could also be an *abbreviation* for the Republic of Niger.

*Be **crude**.*

Naauw intended to *sit at the tip* of the great boulder…*sip at the tit* of the huge rock? Okay, it's tasteless—but it is also memorable.

Does this ring a bell? "Your life is a never-ending torrent of choices. You can choose to do nothing more than hoard and protect your possessions, eat, drink, shag 'n' shut-eye, floating like a day-old turd in a toxic tank." Sure, such language is offensive, but the coarse vulgarity stuck in your mind. It got your attention. And that, dear reader, was my intention…

By the way those words were written by Nero—page 24?

What was the context—the bigger picture—of bare, ragged-arsed essentials?

What are three power habits: "do, do, do," "go, go, go" and…?

*Use **double meanings**.*

After you understand the *Sound* System, having learned the basics and practiced, you will find that it is a very sound system. You'll also hear the sounds in your mind's ear, or with Panasonic or Sony.

Yumm is about memory matters, because memory matters.

Theghn and Naauw; Naauw A'Daze and Yest A'Daze.

Yesterday's romance…an affair to remember?

Memory forgets, but don't forget memory.

Your days are numbered.

She is Modern Man.

Ozone.

Rut.

*Be **dumb.***

If the cupboard is bare, there ain't no supper.

Learning to walk weren't no cakewalk, neither.

Imagine that you intend to make the hole of a doughnut?

Please remain seated, tighten your seat belt, rise and pay…with attention.

Encode.

B4 and the Oh-Zone R not 1, though you and *me* R.

Exaggerate.

Whose vitamin-enriched, mineral-enhanced, energy-boosted, turbo-charged, steak-'n'-strawberry hyper-chunks were under the sink?

Make your impressions huge or tiny, powerful or puny, dazzling or dull, fluorescent, incandescent, psychedelic. Obscene, ribald. Gruesome or funny. Just do it; link and organize. LO and behold.

Group and sort.

by abbreviation: AA, AAA, A1, A4

into parts of the abdomen: stomach, intestines, duodenum (to remember these, use an acronym: sid)

into aberrations: bestiality, pedophilia, sadomasochism (to remember these, use an acrostic: beasts pervert sex)

by ability;

by abnormalities;

by Aboriginals;

alphabetically: at, bat, cat, d   (acdeeegiiiiLlMMmmnnnoorrttUuYy would not be appropriate—*Yumm* is better)

by extremes: aardvark to zymurgy; from working an abacus to fastening a zipper

Use *malapropisms*.

This is when words are comically confused with similar-sounding words:

dismember your pals

expectorate to remember

Harold (or harrowed) be thy name

Give data meaning.

To remember pals is easy. If you understand it—if it has meaning—then the content of that short word becomes truly unforgettable.

Isn't yum about jelly-beans and peanut butter, about being young and care-free? And *Yumm...*?

Create memory bites.

Get set, get, F2, M2, glue and review, is a step-by-step, bit-by-bit, bite-by-bite program. It breaks information into easily actionable chunks, such as 49091092-3875 into 4909, 1092, and 3875.

Baderdien into Dean and Larder.

Novelty has value.

Use red-coats to make things:

bold: PALS & GUTs

crude: use four-letter words…like your mind

different: first the think, then the thing
                astrothaut and cosmothaut
                Cings of the Klassroom
                pay…with attention
                Killer Krumpets

silly: Would Theghn have had a surname? McGinty, at that?

Introduce order.

Yumm is ordered; NmMmMnn ytYlftirirdgaeo eceiiou U is not.

Imagine if the pages of the *little red book* weren't in numerical order, but just printed at random: page 10 was followed by page 23 or 59 or xvii?

The cover upside down, and in the middle…?

Organize.

nmMmMnn ytYlftirirdgaeo eceiiou U is disorganized.

Use your presence of mind to hang those keys on the key rack.

[Be aware of the original time, or place, or mood. This is a form of association. Imagine that while you were standing at your front door, you thought of something to be done. Later you couldn't recall what that was. Go back to the front door; the association that caused that thought originally will probably come back to you.]

*Make information **outstanding***:

Peat, peat, and more peat didn't fit in at all; it didn't make sense; it seemed to be completely out of context. It stood out; that made it memorable.

"From now on, you will support your memory…by design, on purpose, consciously, deliberately, with intention, in cold blood, for life."

Look for pattern:

Mary Johns and John Maree

795 4295 or 345 7652

From now on
henceforth and forevermore
you will give your memory
ongoing **respect, trust,** and **encouragement.**
You will **support** your memory with **love**
by design
on purpose
consciously
deliberately
with intention
in cold blood
for life.

to remember people and their names
we should
get set
get
M2
F2
glue
review

Play on words.

Do you mind?

May I pick your brain?

Presence, presents, gifts and present;

"Our mind's eye" and "our eyes' mind"?

Little cannot exist alone. Nothing can exist alone.

Pun.

A pun is the use of words to exploit double meanings for humorous effect:

And that, as a matter of fact, is the fact of the matter.

What is mind? It doesn't matter.

What is matter? Never mind.

Repeat and review.

Repetition is crucial to learning, knowing, and memory. Go back to what you want to remember—*peat, peat, and more peat.* Review, revise, go over, get feed-back, test yourself. And remember….because

RE-PETITION
RE-PETITION
RE-PETITION
RE-PETITION
RE-PETITION
RE-PETITION
RE-PETITION
RE-PETITION
is essential to effective re-calling and
re-collecting.

Create rhymes/jingles/slogans.

To play tennis or to say Dennis;

Loyal pals attract exciting gals;

Use *Yumm* to find your mind;

Memory is the heart of mind;

Emotion makes memorable;

If it's to be, it's up to me;

It is true, it is up to you.

*Use **spoonerisms**.*

These are the "accidental" changing-over of the initial sounds of words so as to form a ludicrous combination.

Instead of "pick your brain," what about "may I brick your pane" or "prick your bane". If poor memory is your bane, could *Yumm* be the prick?

Understand.

nmMmMytYlftirirdgaeoeceiiouU is neither understandable nor memorable. Your Unlimited, Magnificent Memory is both memorable and understandable.

What is a gospel?

*Be **unusual**.*

Name a rock that burns?

What is the spouse atop the Royal House?

What are the five senses called in *Yumm*-babble?

Wisecracks are also memorable.

Oh, that reminds me, Aunt Mabel is using a spoon to feed her new kitten. Her neighbor loves the little animal. She calls it Cooking Fat.

It's never too late to create a memorable life.

29

An Overview

Only during the last few decades have we, the *Wise Ones,* become sufficiently advanced to be able to start unraveling the workings of our own minds and memory. This ongoing investigation will constantly enrich and improve our understanding of ourselves and how we experience the world.

Further, we are in the midst of enormous individual and global change. The old thinking of looking "out there" for support, of "I am owed; protect me; you must help me," is giving way to taking charge of our own lives. The power we have been seeking "out there" must lie within ourselves. As with everything else, we need to understand in order to make changes. New thinking requires an awareness of the old thinking. The tone of the new thinking is "I must enable myself" and "I must trust myself more."

Acknowledge your success. Miracles are already happening. It takes time and practice for us to learn new ways of thinking. At first, the old ignorant thinking might surface. Be patient with yourself. When we learn a new skill, it is normal and natural that we go forward, slide back a little, and move forward once again. When you are learning something new, and the old pattern returns, are you going to give up, muttering "Hey, this doesn't work"? Or will you assert "Okay, I'm moving in the right direction; there's improvement; I'll try it again"?

Little that we human beings do, or fail to do, is unintentional. It might not be conscious, but at some deep level we do have a reason. Mostly we act because of our unique ability to envision in our minds what doesn't yet exist in reality. We want to achieve a desired result. We all have the talent to recognize what could be—to "see" in advance. The power to invent in our minds is called creative imagination. To be truly practical, imagination must be put to worthwhile use.

This miraculous aspect of mind allowed Man to exploit fire and ride the wheel, to settle the Old World and discover the New, to invent the printing press and the personal computer, and to develop the Internet. Ingenuity produced every contraption that makes our lives easier and better. Insight and inspiration devised every tool we use to probe the remotest depths and the farthest reaches.

And the best people in any field are the ones who use their imagination to dream anew and create afresh. They try out and apply their ideas—concepts they haven't thought of before. The process of improving memory is much the same as that of creating in imagination: actively searching for a connection and forging a link between two previously unconnected ideas.

The past is in our minds. Theghn and Ago are gone. Naauw lives at this time. The time we are feeling is right now. This is the instant we are experiencing. What we are thinking and doing at the moment is laying the foundation for tomorrow. We can't do anything yesterday, and we can't do anything tomorrow. We can only do something today. In fact, we can do it only at this very instant. So this precise blip in time is the point at which to make the decision.

Just take the first step, however small it is. The tiniest beginning will make a difference. *Make it your intention to pay…with attention.* Be consistent and persistent. Don't forget…you and *me* R 1. See on your inner screen, be of sound mind, smell that perfect red rose, taste the hole in the doughnut, touch the sky…SST. Get involved…laugh, cry, experience, feel. *Trust in and have fun with your pals.* And don't forget the repetition. Review her name: It is Mabel Peat-Peat and her number is 345 7652. Her Irish nephew hates her new pet. He calls it a fooking cat.

Without your universal, mighty mind the world wouldn't exist for you. Without your unlimited, magnificent memory you wouldn't be able to make any sense of the stuff "out there." You couldn't respond to the glow of a sunrise over the grasslands, the smell of wood-smoke, the sour taste of a lemon, the romance of a full moon reflected off the ocean, the touch of a loved one…the chirp of a robin.

Stretch yourself through self-enhancement and self-renewal. To expand your memory is to extend your mind. Relax, and have a good time.

Trust in and have fun with your pals.

That old song by Leo Robin will take on a whole new significance:

Thanks for the memory…

P.S. Who wrote "that old song"?

And what was the name of the song?

What was the name of that song?

Could you repeat that?

…and again!

…and again!

…and again!

Once again,

I salute you.

978-0-595-33918-1
0-595-33918-2